VOICE OF
THE PEOPLE

*The Royal Institute of International Affairs is an independent body which promotes the rigorous study of international questions and does not express opinions of its own. The opinions expressed in this publication are the responsibility of the author.*

# VOICE OF THE PEOPLE

The European Parliament in the 1990s

Julie Smith

THE ROYAL INSTITUTE OF
INTERNATIONAL AFFAIRS
**European Programme**

© Royal Institute of International Affairs, 1995

Published in Great Britain in 1995 by the Royal Institute of International Affairs, Chatham House, 10 St James's Square, London SW1Y 4LE (Charity Registration No. 208 223).

Distributed worldwide by The Brookings Institution, 1775 Massachusetts Avenue, Northwest, Washington, DC 20036-2188, USA.

All rights reserved. No part of this publication may be reproduced, stored in a retrieval system, or transmitted by any other means without the prior written permission of the copyright holder. Please direct all inquiries to the publishers.

**British Library Cataloguing in Publication Data**
A CIP catalogue record for this book is available from the British Library.

ISBN 0 905031 88 1

Text set in Bembo.
Printed and bound in Great Britain by Redwood Books.

# CONTENTS

| | |
|---|---|
| Foreword | vii |
| Preface | viii |
| Acknowledgments | ix |
| Abbreviations | x |
| **1 Introduction** | **1** |
| **2 European elections – 1979 to 1989** | **6** |
| The rules of the game | 6 |
| Getting the voters interested | 10 |
| The party dimension | 12 |
| Campaigns and issues | 15 |
| Turnout | 17 |
| Results | 18 |
| **3 European elections 1994** | **21** |
| Governmental agenda | 23 |
| The transnational manifestos | 26 |
| Countries | 30 |
| Summary | 53 |
| Austria, Finland and Sweden – a note | 54 |
| **4 The European Parliament** | **60** |
| The Common Assembly – a parliament in search of a role | 61 |
| Background information | 63 |
| How the European Parliament works | 71 |
| The powers of the Parliament | 73 |
| Inter-institutional links | 90 |
| Lobbyists and business | 91 |
| Summary | 92 |

| | |
|---|---|
| **5 Beyond 1996** | **93** |
| Appendix 1: Legislative procedures | 98 |
| Appendix 2: Revisions of rules of procedure | 101 |
| Appendix 3: Committees in the European Parliament | 103 |
| Appendix 4: Tables of votes and seats for Member States | 104 |

# FOREWORD

The European Parliament represents the people of the European Union. Its 626 directly elected Members are their voice in shaping the future of Europe. This book, which reviews the structure of the Parliament as it emerged from the elections of June 1994, is a timely reminder that the voice of the people is growing louder year by year and increasingly bears weight on European politics. The Single European Act and the Treaty on European Union each added to the powers of the European Parliament, making the construction of Europe more accountable. The reforms to be negotiated in 1996 should continue in the same direction.

To be true to our origins and to our ideals, Europe must confirm its democratic identity. Our procedures and proceedings must be open, comprehensible and fair. Our decision and our laws must reflect the will of the people. Parliaments – both the European Parliament and the national parliaments of all our member states – must play a full part in reflecting the will of the people.

The political parties of our old continent must rise to the challenge of shaping Europe anew and of carrying the people of our Union with them in making their democratic choice. And the vast European electorate must be fully informed about the issues and the options that face their representatives.

We cannot go further with European integration without debate. We cannot make progress, if public opinion does not want it. We can no longer confect treaties in secret. I warmly welcome that this debate is taking place in public and in publications. And for the debate to be realistic, we need well-founded analysis and thoughts on the interests and issues and proposals at stake.

This book attempts to do this for the European Parliament and I warmly welcome its contribution to the great debate about our future.

*April 1995*　　　　　　　　　　　　　　　　　　　　　Klaus Hänsch
　　　　　　　　　　　　　　　　　President of the European Parliament

# PREFACE

This book is a revised and expanded second edition of the RIIA Special Paper *Citizens' Europe? The European Elections and the Role of the European Parliament*, which was published in the run-up to the European elections of June 1994. Naturally, Chapter 3, which considers the 1994 elections, has been rewritten in the light of the election campaigns in the twelve existing member states and the referenda in the four Eftan applicant countries. Sections on the European Parliament have also been substantially rewritten to take into account changes since the elections, both those which have arisen as a result of the outcome of the elections and those which have arisen from the new powers the Parliament received under the Maastricht Treaty, but was unable to use prior to the elections. Some of the background material contained in the first edition has been retained, but all the tables have been updated to include changes due to the elections and to enlargement. The book's new title reflects a slight shift of emphasis towards the Parliament and away from the electoral dimension.

*April 1995*                                                               Julie Smith

# ACKNOWLEDGMENTS

This book was prepared within the European Programme at the Royal Institute of International Affairs. The European Programme studies developments throughout the wider Europe, extending to the borders of the former Soviet Union. It aims to stimulate and provoke debate about the political, economic and strategic choices facing the countries of Europe, and to analyse relations between Europe and the rest of the world.

I would like to express warm thanks to all the MEPs and their assistants, Parliament and Commission officials, members of the Permanent Representations to the EU, academics and journalists for all their help over the past year and a half. I am most grateful also to everyone on the European Programme and in the Publications Department of Chatham House for all their efforts in preparing the final version for publication. Any errors are of course my responsibility.

*April 1995* Julie Smith

## The author

The author is Lecturer in Politics at Brasenose College, Oxford, and is currently completing her doctoral dissertation on the European Parliament.

# ABBREVIATIONS

| | |
|---|---|
| CAP | Common Agricultural Policy |
| CDU | Christian Democratic Union (Germany) |
| CFSP | Common Foreign and Security Policy |
| CiU | Catalonian Nationalists |
| COREPER | Committee of Permanent Representatives |
| CSCE | Conference on Security and Cooperation in Europe (now OSCE) |
| CSP | Confederation of Socialist Parties |
| CSU | Christian Social Union (Germany) |
| CSV | Christian Democrats (Luxembourg) |
| D66 | Democracy 66 |
| EC | European Community |
| ECSC | European Coal and Steel Community |
| EDA | Group of the European Democratic Alliance |
| EDG | European Democratic Group |
| EEC | European Economic Community |
| EFTA | European Free Trade Association |
| ELDR | European Liberal, Democrat and Reform |
| EMU | Economic and Monetary Union |
| EN | Europe of the Nations Group |
| EPLP | European Parliamentary Labour Party |
| EPP | European People's Party |
| ERA | Group of the European Radical Alliance |
| ERM | Exchange Rate Mechanism |
| EP | European Parliament |
| EU | European Union |
| Euratom | European Atomic Energy Community |
| FDP | Free Democrat Party (Germany) |

| | |
|---|---|
| FE | Forza Europa Group |
| GATT | General Agreement on Tariffs and Trade |
| Greens | Green Group in the European Parliament |
| IGC | Intergovernmental Conference |
| IU | Izquierda Unida (Spain) |
| JHA | Justice and Home Affairs |
| LSAP | Social Democrats (Luxembourg) |
| MEP | Member of the European Parliament |
| NA | Non-attached |
| NACC | North Atlantic Cooperation Council |
| NATO | North Atlantic Treaty Organization |
| OSCE | Organization for Security and Cooperation in Europe |
| PDS | Party of Democratic Socialism (Germany); Party of the Democratic Left (Italy) |
| PES | Party of European Socialists |
| PP | Popular Party (Spain) |
| PR | Proportional Representation |
| PSOE | Spanish Socialist Party |
| QMV | Qualified Majority Voting |
| RPR | Rally for the Republic (French Gaullists) |
| SEA | Single European Act |
| SPD | Social Democrat Party (Germany) |
| STV | Single transferable vote |
| TEU | Treaty on European Union (Maastricht Treaty) |
| UDF | Union for French Democracy |
| United Left | Confederal Group of the United European Left |
| WEU | Western European Union |

# 1 INTRODUCTION

No parliament is ever given powers; it has to take them. Long convinced of the truth of these words, Members of the European Parliament (MEPs) have always fought to increase their say in European decision-making. The six months following the European elections in June 1994 gave the parliamentarians ample scope to exert their new-found strength. Indeed, in the first plenary week after the elections MEPs rejected legislation on the rather obscure issue of voice telephony partly on the grounds that they would not have enough of a say in subsequent amendments to the legislation. Two days later they came close to rejecting the Council's nominee for the Commission presidency, Jacques Santer. Although that was only a consultative vote, it was enough to show that the incoming Parliament meant business. Then in January 1995, the Members of a European Parliament (EP) enlarged by the entry to the European Union (EU) of Austria, Finland and Sweden formally gave the incoming Commission a vote of confirmation.

The European Parliament of the 1990s has a clear and growing role in the legislative and budgetary processes of the European Union (see Box 1). It now plays an important part in the choice of the EU's executive body, the Commission, and has powers of scrutiny over it as well. Yet parliamentarians argue that these powers are not adequate. In particular, they claim that the existence of a 'democratic deficit' in European decision-making implies a need for further powers for the Parliament. This problem was defined by the EP as the combination of two phenomena: (a) the transfer of powers from the member states to the European Community; and (b) the exercise of these powers at the Community level by institutions other than the European Parliament, even though, before the transfer, the national parliaments held power to pass laws in these areas.[1]

1. European Parliament Report drawn up on behalf of the Committee on Institutional Affairs on the democratic deficit in the European Community: PE 111.236/fin.1, February 1988, pp. 10–11.

> **Box 1: Key changes from the Maastricht Treaty**
>
> **The European Community Pillar**
>
> - Vote of confidence in Commission and Commission Presidency
> - Introduction of co-decision with the Council in certain policy areas
> - Extension of the assent procedure
> - Consultation on the appointment of candidates for the Presidency of the Central bank, members of its Board, the Presidency of the Monetary Institute and members of the Court of Auditors
> - Ombudsman to be appointed by Parliament
> - Parliament may set up temporary committees of enquiry
>
> **The Justice and Home Affairs and Common Foreign and Security Pillars**
>
> - Council and Commission to inform Parliament about activities
> - Parliament may adopt recommendations
> - Parliament has the right to put questions to the Council
>
> *Source*: Compiled from Richard Corbett, *PE\GS 234.93* 30 September 1993.

While the concept of the democratic deficit is not new, it has been exacerbated by recent treaties, particularly the 1987 Single European Act (SEA), which led to an increase in the amount of qualified majority voting (QMV) in the Council of Ministers, and a corresponding decrease in the scope of parliamentary accountability. The introduction, in the Maastricht Treaty, of the co-decision procedure which allows MEPs to veto proposed European legislation has gone some way to overcome the problem. Yet this procedure covers only a limited number of policy areas currently tackled at the European level and exclusively those in the first pillar of the Union.[2] Paradoxically it was the Maastricht Treaty, which aimed to overcome existing problems in European decision-making, and not the Single European

---

2. The Treaty on European Union created a 'pillar structure' under which the three existing communities, the Coal and Steel Community, the Atomic Energy Community and the European Economic Community (officially renamed the European Community in the treaty) are brought together as the 'European Community pillar', while matters relating to foreign and security policy, and to justice and home affairs are dealt with under the provisions of the second and third pillars respectively.

Act, that led voters to articulate dissent about the powers of the European Community.

Parliament's role in the Common Foreign and Security policy (CFSP) and Justice and Home Affairs (JHA) pillars of the European Union is even more limited. Decisions in these areas are made on a largely intergovernmental basis and increased cooperation in these fields does mean that more activities are now dealt with by national executives acting jointly in the Council of Ministers. National parliaments can hold ministers from their own countries accountable for their activity, but not the Council as a whole. In policy areas which fall under the provisions of the first pillar, the gap is partly filled by the EP; in the other two pillars it is not. Admittedly, the EP has the right of consultation and information from the Council Presidency and the Commission on major questions in these policy areas, but since Council takes its decisions behind closed doors, scrutiny and accountability are extremely limited.

With two representatives on the working group preparing for the intergovernmental conference (IGC) scheduled for 1996, to review the Maastricht procedures, the incoming European Parliament now has a chance to push to increase its powers still further. Only a matter of months after enlargement to include Austria, Finland and Sweden, and with the prospect of further enlargement in the short to medium term, MEPs have a more important weapon than previously to use in their call for major reforms. The Eftan enlargement negotiations fudged major institutional questions; any changes, such as the addition of one member of the College of Commissioners for each of the acceding states, and the method of allocating weighted votes in the Council of Ministers, were incremental. While such an approach could be taken in the case of four small, economically and politically stable states, it avoids certain fundamental issues.[3] If the European Union is to function well, inter-institutional relationships need to be redefined to reflect the possibility of a Union of twenty or more members. Many different scenarios exist, partly depending on one's view of what the EU is or should be. One approach which the EP might plausibly argue for is a greater approximation to a parliamentary Europe. Various scenarios as to what this might entail are put forward in Chapter 5 of this volume.

3. The negotiations and institutional arrangements covered four countries, including Norway until its citizens finally voted 'No' in a referendum on accession on 28 November 1994.

It is clear that the European Parliament is a dynamic institution whose role in the Union is likely to increase in the coming years. Despite the growing importance of the Parliament, voter interest in the 1994 European elections was even less than in previous years, with average turnout down to 58.3%. Several states saw a re-nationalization of the election campaigns, even though there were strong reasons for a more European approach to the elections than had been the case in the past. That this should be the case despite the increased powers of the European Parliament, and the fact that voters in some countries had the opportunity to vote on European issues for the first time since the Maastricht Treaty, raises serious questions about the role of the European Parliament and its claims to democratic legitimacy.[4]

Many of the problems surrounding the Maastricht Treaty emerged because of a failure by national governments to take the opinions of their publics into consideration. Although the rhetoric suggests that the 1996 IGC will ensure more public debate before decisions are finally taken, the best opportunity to discuss some of the themes was in the European election campaigns.[5] For various reasons, some of which are explored in subsequent chapters, this opportunity was not taken up. We argue that failure to discuss such issues of fundamental importance to the lives of Europe's citizens contributed to the lack of interest in the elections and suggest ways in which the Parliament can help interest the electorate in European affairs in the future.

Chapter 2 gives an overview of the first three sets of elections to the European Parliament, noting the tendency for national actors and issues to predominate. Chapter 3 looks at the 1994 elections, considering national and transnational manifestos and the differences in campaigning across the Union. It concludes with a brief summary of the impact of the results in national and European terms. Chapter 4 considers where this leaves the European Parliament in the mid-1990s. The role of the EP and the way it

---

4. Only in France, Denmark and Ireland, where referenda were held, could voters express their views on the Treaty.
5. It is interesting to note that in the week of the vote on Jacques Santer, representatives of the Council as well as the President of the European Parliament, Klaus Hänsch, and the President-designate of the Commission himself all stressed the need to bring Europe closer to the people. See for example European Parliament, *Strasbourg Notebook*, 20 and 21 July 1994 (PE177.797, PE177.796 and PE 177.798).

functions are outlined, with an assessment of how its activities have been affected by the outcome of the 1994 elections and the introduction of the provisions of the Maastricht Treaty. In Chapter 5 we consider what the EP can do to bring Europe closer to its citizens. Finally we look at the issues which are likely to be on the EP's agenda for the 1996 IGC and offer certain policy suggestions of our own.

# 2 EUROPEAN ELECTIONS – 1979 TO 1989

Direct elections to the European Parliament took place for the first time in June 1979. The experience of those, and of subsequent elections in 1984 and 1989, was of domestically focused campaigns, with little attention paid to wider European issues. Interest among voters and national politicians was limited and this was reflected in low turnout across the Community. The campaigns and results in the various member states were a testimony to national preoccupations, with protest voting on a large scale and the opportunity arising for new and small parties to perform well. Apart from transnational manifestos, there was little campaigning at the European level. The impression was thus of a set of simultaneous national elections to a common body rather than of a single election. Most commentators concur with Karlheinz Reif's conclusion that these elections should be seen as second-order, more like local than general elections.[6] This chapter gives an overview of the elections, looking at campaigns, turnout and results.

## The rules of the game

Although the European Parliament has been directly elected since 1979, it has never been elected under a common electoral system. As early as 1951, the possibility was raised in the Treaty of Paris for elections to the Common Assembly, as the EP was originally known.[7] The subsequent Treaties of Rome (1957) establishing the European Economic Community (EEC) and

---

6. See Karlheinz Reif, 'National Electoral Cycles and European Elections, 1979 and 1984', *Electoral Studies*, vol. 3, 1984, pp. 244–55 and Karlheinz Reif (ed.), *Ten European Elections – 1979/81 and 1984 – Campaigns and Results* (Aldershot: Gower, 1985).
7. Article 138(3) of the Treaty of Paris (1957) establishing the European Coal and Steel Community states: 'The Assembly shall draw up proposals for elections by direct universal suffrage in accordance with a uniform procedure in all member states.'

the European Atomic Energy Community (Euratom) and the Maastricht Treaty (1992) all call for elections by direct universal suffrage.

Broad agreement amongst member states that there should be direct elections has never been translated into agreement on an identical system; there was a belief among leaders that in principle there should be a uniform system, but they all added that any such system should be based on their own national system.[8] In a classic compromise it was accepted that 'uniformity was not synonymous with identity'.[9] As long as the procedures adopted in the member states gave 'universal, free, equal and secret elections' they would satisfy the criteria for direct elections. The thorny problem of securing a genuinely uniform procedure was then left to the directly elected Parliament to solve. Attempts have been made to introduce a common system, but so far without success. The De Gucht Report which was adopted by the EP in March 1993 represents a step in that direction, but it is not certain that it will overcome the hurdle of the Council, which has the power to settle the question.[10] In any case, it is debatable whether even the De Gucht Report actually gives a uniform procedure; members of the new Commission, as well as certain MEPs, think it does not.[11]

De Gucht's proposal provides a set of guidelines for member states to follow, the main requirement being that there must be some element of proportionality in the system. Britain would have to modify its rules for European elections, but the other states would be able to keep their individual systems as they now stand. Differences over the use of national or regional multi-member constituencies, the question of whether voters

8. See the Patijn Report on this, European Parliament Document 386/74.
9. This idea was first put forward in the Dehousse Report of 1960.
10. Prior to the De Gucht Report, the Seitlinger Report, passed by the EP on 10 March 1982, was the nearest the EC had come to a uniform procedure, but even that did not offer a genuinely uniform system; in any case, it did not get through the Council. In 1992 the British Liberal Democrats took the EP to the European Court of Justice for failing in its duty to produce a uniform electoral system. Although this action failed, the Advocate-General actually supported the grievance, but felt that the *party* did not have a right to bring a case before the Court. Thus, the Liberal Democrats may put pressure on the Parliament to bring a case against the Council if the latter fails to adopt the de Gucht Report.
11. E.g. Mr Santer answering questions from one of the party groups prior to the vote on his nomination in July 1994 and Mr Oreja in the hearings of the Institutional Affairs Committee, 4 January 1995 (author's private notes).

## Table 1: Electoral rules in European elections

| Country | No. of seats (1994) | No. of const. | Electoral system | Choice of candidate | Compulsory voting | Work or rest-day voting |
|---|---|---|---|---|---|---|
| Belgium | 25 | 4[a] | Proportional: regional lists | Yes from party list | Yes | Rest |
| Denmark | 16 | 1 | Proportional: national list | Yes from party list | No | Work |
| Germany | 99 | 1 | Proportional: regional lists[b] | No – strict party list | No | Rest |
| Greece | 25 | 1 | Proportional: national list | No – strict party list | Yes | Rest |
| Spain | 64 | 1 | Proportional: national list | No – strict party list | No | Rest |
| France | 87 | 1 | Proportional: national list | No – strict party list | No | Rest |
| Ireland | 15 | 4 | Proportional: single transferable vote (STV) | Yes – no list | No | Work[c] |
| Italy | 87 | 5 | Proportional: regional lists | Yes – party list, but also preference votes | No | Rest |
| Luxembourg | 6 | 1 | Proportional: national list | Yes, open lists | Yes | Rest |
| Netherlands | 31 | 1 | Proportional: national list | Yes from party list | No | Work |
| Portugal | 25 | 1 | Proportional: national list | No – strict party list | No | Rest |
| UK | 87 | 85[d] | Plurality in GB | Yes – no list | No | Work |

*Notes*:
[a] As of June 1994, there are to be four constituencies, but only three electoral colleges, a Flemish one which will elect 14 members, a Francophone one electing 10 members and a one-member German-speaking one.
[b] Parties may present lists on a Land rather than a national basis, however. The CDU presents lists in all the Länder except Bavaria and CSU presents a list only in Bavaria.
[c] The 1984 election took place on a Sunday.
[d] 84 single-member constituencies in Great Britain and one 3-member constituency in N. Ireland where members are elected by Single Transferable Vote (STV).

*Source*: Compiled by the author from various sources including her own unpublished MPhil thesis, *The European Parliament and Direct Elections* (1993) and T.T. Mackie, *Europe Votes 3 – European Parliamentary Election Results 1989* (Aldershot: Dartmouth Publishing Company Ltd, 1990).

should be granted any choice of candidate or simply choose between rigid party lists, and variations in thresholds for representation could all persist under the proposals of De Gucht.

Table 1, which lays out the electoral rules in force in the twelve member states in 1994 (which differ little from previous elections), clearly demonstrates how far provisions for the elections differ between states. Eleven states used some form of proportional representation (PR): eight countries have adopted proportional systems with national constituencies (although one of these countries has regional lists); three have regional constituencies. Great Britain, which had a single-member plurality system, is the exception. Whilst these differences may not appear to be particularly important, in reality the absence of identical electoral laws does create difficulties.

The lack of a common electoral system led to the claim after the 1979 elections that it was difficult to view European elections as transnational rather than as simultaneous national elections.[12] Yet the absence of Europe-wide media is far more significant in this respect – national and local media tend to raise national and local issues respectively, but there is no comparable arena for coverage of Europe-wide issues. The absence of a common electoral system would, in fact, become more apparent if elections were held to choose the College of Commissioners or the Commission President. In that case it would be very difficult to field a common slate of candidates if Britain were determined to retain its electoral system.

In practical terms, however, Britain's plurality system does have an important distortionary impact: a minor shift in voting patterns in Britain can dramatically alter the numbers of seats held by the British parties, and in turn by the party groups in the European Parliament.[13] In 1979, for example, the Conservatives, fresh from victory in the general election, won 60 seats, Labour only 17; by 1989, the position had shifted dramatically, with Labour holding 45 seats and the Conservatives 32, making Labour the largest single party in the EP, even though it did not have the greatest support in percentage terms. This situation was further exaggerated following the 1994

---

12. See for example Valentine Herman and Juliet Lodge, 'Direct Elections to the European Parliament: A Supranational Perspective', *European Journal of Political Research*, vol. 8, 1980, pp. 45–62.
13. See Andrew Duff, 'Building a Parliamentary Europe', *Government and Opposition*, vol. 29, no. 2, spring 1994.

elections and, as Chapter 4 demonstrates, it has had a major impact on the party's influence in the Parliament.

Finally, differences in electoral regulations also affect turnout. As Table 2 shows, figures in Belgium, Greece and Luxembourg, where voting is compulsory, are much higher than anywhere else apart from Italy, where voting is quasi-compulsory.[14] Turnout is also affected by the coincidence of domestic (general or local) and European elections. Indeed, it was partly a desire for high turnout in European elections that permitted simultaneity of elections, but the trade-off for increased turnout is an even greater emphasis on national issues.

### Getting the voters interested

The expectation that high turnout would confer democratic legitimacy on both the Parliament and the Community led to concerted attempts to mobilize voters. Prior to the first set of direct elections in 1979, Martin Bangemann[15] put Parliament's case for high turnout thus:

> Inadequate mobilization of the public and a consequent poor voter turnout for the direct elections will entail the danger that the Parliament's influence and powers are not strengthened but weakened.[16]

The Commission was also anxious to increase voter awareness of the Community and its institutions through the elections. In order to heighten the effect, it was decided to have a single, non-partisan campaign, headed by the Commission, with the aim of raising voter awareness about the elections and increasing turnout. The resulting *European Elections Information Programmes* had some common organizational features, although they were implemented on a national basis in the run-up to the political campaigns. Since the elections were put back from 1978 to 1979, there was an added problem of maintaining awareness for a whole year.

14. Although not legally compulsory, voting is called a 'civic duty' in the Italian constitution and failure to vote is thought to have adverse consequences, particularly when seeking employment.
15. At the time a Member of the European Parliament, Bangemann has also been an FDP minister in the German government and is now a European Commissioner.
16. Martin Bangemann, 'Preparations for Direct Elections in the Federal Republic of Germany', *Common Market Law Review*, vol. 15, 1978, pp. 321–38.

Table 2: Turnout in European Parliament elections 1979-1994

|  | 1979 % | 1981 % | 1984 % | 1987 % | 1989 % | 1994 % | Average[b] % |
|---|---|---|---|---|---|---|---|
| Belgium[a] | 91.4 | — | 92.2 | — | 90.7 | 90.7 | 91.2 |
| Denmark | 47.8 | — | 52.4 | — | 46.2 | 52.5 | 49.7 |
| Germany | 65.7 | — | 56.8 | — | 62.3 | 60.1 | 61.2 |
| Greece[a] | — | 78.6 | 77.2 | — | 79.9 | 71.2 | 76.7 |
| Spain | — | — | — | 68.9 | 54.6 | 59.6 | 61.0 |
| France | 60.7 | — | 56.7 | — | 48.7 | 52.7 | 54.7 |
| Ireland | 63.6 | — | 47.6 | — | 68.3 | 44.0 | 55.9 |
| Italy | 84.9 | — | 83.4 | — | 81.0 | 74.8 | 81.0 |
| Lux[a] | 88.9 | — | 88.8 | — | 87.4 | 88.5 | 88.4 |
| NL | 57.8 | — | 50.6 | — | 47.2 | 35.6 | 47.8 |
| Portugal | — | — | — | 72.6 | 51.2 | 35.6 | 53.1 |
| UK | 32.3 | — | 32.6 | — | 36.2 | 36.4 | 34.4 |
| EC | 65.9[c] | — | 63.8[d] | — | 62.8[e] | 58.3 | 62.9[f] |

*Notes*:
Unweighted figures used. Weighting gives slightly lower turnout figures.
[a] Voting is compulsory.
[b] The average figures refer to the average turnout for the elections of 1979, 1984, 1989 and 1994, except for Greece, where they refer to 1981, 1984, 1989 and 1994, and Spain and Portugal, where they refer to 1987, 1989 and 1994.
[c] The average for the EC9.
[d] The average for the EC10.
[e] The average for the EC12.
[f] The figure is an average based on all the elections which have occurred between 1979 and 1994, i.e. four elections except for Spain and Portugal.

*Sources*: European Parliament, *Results and Elected Members* (Provisional Edition 15 June 1994) and *Info Memo 'Election Special' No. 1* (Brussels: EP – Directorate General for Information and Public Relations, 1994).

It is not clear exactly how beneficial such campaigns were: awareness of the EP and the elections did indeed rise in the pre-election period, but *Eurobarometer* data suggest that voter awareness is highly cyclical anyway, peaking just after the 1979, just before the 1984 and just after the 1989 elections at 66%, 75% and 71% respectively.[17] Moreover, people who said they were aware of the Information Programmes were not always favourably impressed.

17. The European Commission regularly publishes opinion poll data in the form of *Eurobarometer*.

The experiment has not been repeated since 1979 and turnout has changed little over the years, declining very slightly on average, but varying from country to country.[18] Public awareness of the Parliament and the elections has tended to be low, rising only in the run-up to the elections (and also during the first Danish referendum campaign in 1992). In view of this it is perhaps not surprising that European elections have low levels of voter mobilization.

## The party dimension

Right from the start, members sat with political allies in the EP, not in national groups (see Chart 1).[19] In the run-up to the first direct elections, links between the various political 'families' were strengthened as Christian Democrats, Socialists and Liberals set up European party federations. Subsequently these federations have all formally become parties, partly as a result of the Maastricht Treaty, which is the first treaty to include mention of European political parties, leading to hopes that money might be available to fund such parties.[20] The transnational parties are composed of parties from EU and other European states. They are technically distinct from the various party Internationals, such as the Socialist International, which predate them, and from the party groups which sit in the European Parliament. However, members of the main party groups in the EP tend also to be members of the transnational parties.[21] Whilst the party federations produced manifestos for the first three sets of European elections, campaigns were typically fought by the constituent national parties, with little or no transnational campaigning.

The transnational parties are gradually playing an increased role elsewhere in European politics, such as in the pre-summit meetings in the run-

---

18. As noted in Chapter 3, there was a general campaign aimed at getting the voters out in Germany in 1994. Turnout fell slightly compared with the 1989 elections, but was above the European average.
19. As Jacobs *at al.* note, this was the first time such an arrangement had happened: e.g. members of the Parliamentary Assembly of the Council of Europe only began to sit with political allies in 1964. Francis Jacobs, Richard Corbett and Michael Shackleton, *The European Parliament* (London: Longman, 3rd edition forthcoming, 1995), p. 57.
20. Treaty on European Union, Article 138a.
21. The chief exceptions in this regard are Danish and British MEPs who, along with some French Members, sit with the Group of the European Peoples Party in the EP as allied members, even though the national parties are not members of the transnational parties.

Chart 1: The European Parliament, 28 April 1994

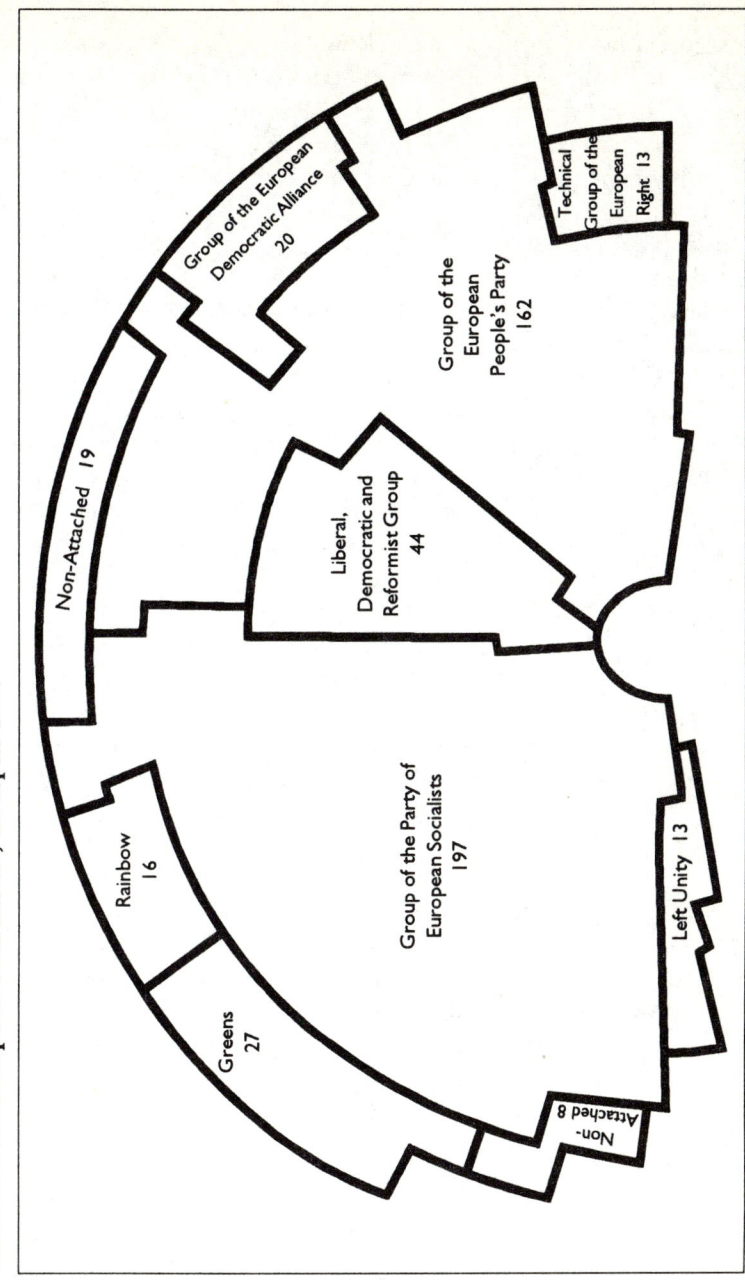

Source: European Parliament.

up to European Council meetings. Thus, for example, the Christian Democrat heads of government met two days before the Corfu European Summit in June 1994 to try to reach an agreement on their nominee for the Commission President. Socialists did likewise, giving a sense of the growing importance of political links at the European level.

*Transnational party federations*
Socialist politicians were the first to react to the likely introduction of European elections, setting up the *Confederation of Socialist Parties (CSP)* in 1974. They were not able to commit themselves wholeheartedly to a federal goal, in large part because French, British and Danish socialists espoused different views of Europe from those of the other socialist parties. Nor were closer links even seen as a possibility in the near future: the first president of the CSP, Wilhelm Droscher, declared in 1974 that 'the development of a European Socialist Party is not a realistic possibility in the near future. This would create insoluble problems for the national parties.'[22] In fact, the Federation voted to call itself a party – the *Party of European Socialists (PES)* – in November 1992.

The CSP produced an 'Appeal to the Electorate' in 1979 and more formal manifestos in 1984 and 1989. The intention was that the manifesto should act as a guideline for national manifestos, not replace them. Nevertheless, the British and Danish parties opted out of some aspects of all the documents. Given the national focus of campaigns, the role of the CSP, like that of other transnational party federations, has been limited.

The *European People's Party (EPP)*, set up in 1976, was founded on the basis of Christian Democracy and with a commitment to the goal of a federal Europe. That commitment has contributed to divisions among the parties of the centre and centre-right: Christian Democrats have tended to be members of the EPP, whereas Conservatives, notably from Britain, Spain and Denmark, and French Gaullists have favoured looser parliamentary groupings. MEPs from the first three of those countries were originally members of the *European Democratic Group (EDG)*, a much weaker body than the EPP. Although members of the EDG sat together as a group in the European Parliament, there was never any attempt to have a common manifesto or common campaign strategies. However, the situation altered

---

22. Cited in S. Henig (ed.), *Political Parties in the European Community* (London: George Allen and Unwin, 1979), p. 285.

significantly during the 1989/94 parliament. Immediately after the June 1989 election, the Spanish Popular Party (PP) left the EDG to join the EPP. Since the number of the British and Danish Conservative MEPs had been dramatically reduced from 49 to 34, the EDG's weight in Parliament was weakened and it became a virtually irrelevant force. From April 1992, these MEPs sat with the Group of the EPP as 'allied members'.

The EPP's manifestos for the first three elections stated principles rather than putting forward specific short-term policies, stressing, for example, the desire for increased powers for the EP, a federal Europe and an extension of the conciliation procedure. This was partly due to the fact that, even before the aforementioned changes in membership and party links, there were political differences within the EPP. Christian Democrats in Italy and the Benelux countries are more inclined to work with Socialist parties than are the German CDU (Christian Democratic Union) and, especially, its sister party, the Bavarian CSU (Christian Socialist Union). As with the Socialists, the EPP has tended to support the activities of national member parties rather than conduct a single transnational campaign.

The *Federation of European Liberals, Democrats and Reformers (ELDR)*, established in 1976, voted to become the *European Liberal Democrat and Reform Party* in December 1993. The party is probably the most heterogeneous of the main European parties as it encompasses the relatively left-wing British Liberal Democrats as well as more free-market groups like the German Free Democrats (FDP). Internal tensions were revealed in the opposition of British Liberals to the membership of the right-wing French Parti Républicain on the grounds that it was not a 'liberal' party. The differences between the parties have made thrashing out a common manifesto difficult.

In 1993, the Green parties formed a transnational party federation, the *European Federation of Green Parties*, comprising 35 parties extending as far east as Ukraine. Although Green parties stood in earlier elections, they did not produce a common manifesto until the 1994 election.

## Campaigns and issues

Although European elections are contemporaneous,[23] they take place at different points in the national electoral cycles of the member states. In some

---

23. The elections are actually spread over a four-day period to accommodate different national traditions concerning work-day and rest-day voting.

countries the elections take place mid-term; in others straight after a general election, during the 'honeymoon period'; in others, they coincide with national elections. As for local elections, the timing of European elections within the national cycle affects the results and turnout. The nature of the campaigns also differs within and between the member states as they respond to specific national events. It is important to consider the political background in each state at the time of the elections in order to understand the nature of the campaigns and the outcomes of the elections.

When European elections have coincided with national elections, there has been a much greater focus on national rather than European issues. This was the case in Luxembourg, where national and European elections have been scheduled to coincide on each occasion.[24] The Greek experience in 1981 provides an interesting example of voters discriminating between elections. National elections coincided with European elections in 1981,[25] and although the main thrust of the campaign was domestic, the results in the national and European polls differed quite significantly. The strongly pro-EC New Democracy won 4% fewer votes in the European election than in the national, while the Socialist group, Pasok, which had originally been hostile to the EC but gradually shifted to support it, went down by 8%. The pro-EC Communist KKE-es vote went up compared with the national results; that of the anti-EC Communist Party KKE did not.

When campaigns have taken place at times of government instability or national crises, domestic affairs have again tended to predominate. Thus, in 1989, the Italian parties played down their differences concerning certain aspects of European integration in order to maximize their vote in the national elections. In the Netherlands, little attention was paid to the European elections in that year, because a general election was pending and parties were unwilling to jeopardize ties with potential national coalition partners through their attitudes to European affairs. The result was a lacklustre campaign, characterized by apathy on the part of voters and parties, and turnout down from 50.6% to 47.2%.

24. Luxembourg has a five-year fixed electoral cycle and so it was decided in 1979 that the two elections should be scheduled to occur on the same day, since national elections were already due that year. This decision was made for practical reasons of cost, but also to give symbolic support to the European elections.
25. Greece held European elections for the first time in October 1981 following accession to the Union in January of that year.

European elections have frequently been treated like national opinion polls on the state of political parties. In 1979, for instance, the result in France was taken as an indicator for the 1981 Presidential election, while the British Labour Party used the 1989 election as a plebiscite on ten years of Conservative government. In such cases, little emphasis is placed on European issues and there is nothing to suggest to voters that European elections matter in terms of results at the European level.

Denmark has been a special case, with party alignments differing between European and national elections. Parties hostile to the EC came together as the People's Movement Against the Common Market in the first three European elections, which could best be characterized as reruns of the 1972 accession referendum. Danish voters thus had the opportunity to express an opinion on European integration, at least in terms of whether or not they favoured EC membership. In spite of this, turnout in these elections was lower in Denmark than in any member state apart from Britain. Thus giving voters a choice on European issues may not increase voter mobilization; it is desirable, however, since it allows people to register views on issues which in other states tend to cause divisions within rather than between parties.

The problem seems to be that questions concerning the future of European integration are generally addressed only in countries where there is little difference between the main parties on such issues; thus scant impetus is given to debate which might arouse interest in the elections. None of the elections could be said to have been fought on transnational issues, such as, for example, European environmental policy. This can be attributed to the fact that national parties and parliaments and, perhaps equally importantly, the national media tend to dictate the political agenda. Since many national politicians jealously try to guard the legislative powers to which they still lay claim, there has been a marked reluctance to make voters aware of the growing role of the European Parliament and hence of the European elections. Moreover, unlike most national elections, European Parliament elections do not result in a change of government; the most that can be achieved is a change in the political complexion of the EP. This may well have a disincentive effect on potential voters.

## Turnout

As the data in Table 2 show, turnout in the European Parliament elections has been fairly low across the whole Community. In all cases it was below the level in national elections (with the exception of Luxembourg in 1979 and 1984). There are obviously wide disparities in the figures, for the reasons noted above.

However, although turnout has been low by West European standards, it has not been low by comparison with the United States. In the off-year of 1986 turnout in Congressional elections fell to 33.4%. Even Presidential elections have seen low turnout, with a postwar high of 62.6% in 1960 and only 55% in the 1992 poll.[26] Nor is turnout very different from that recorded in local elections in the EU, with the marked exception of Denmark, which has high voter mobilization in national and local elections (on average 84.5% in national elections compared with only 48.8% in European elections, lower than in any state bar Great Britain).[27]

Turnout fell gradually over the course of three European elections, in particular in France, Spain, Portugal and the Netherlands. For Spain and Portugal there are quite plausible explanations for this: in 1987 both countries had simultaneous domestic and European elections; in 1989 this was not the case.

## Results

In general the elections were not fought on a Community-wide basis and the results were primarily determined by domestic factors. There was frequently scope for protest voting, and large parties, both government and opposition, fared badly (with the Netherlands the only real exception to this pattern). In particular, the elections have given parties of the far right and the Greens a significant boost, frequently helping them to achieve national prominence and subsequently to build on such success at the national elections.

As mentioned earlier, such results have led to the conclusion that the elections could best be viewed as second-order. An important part of this claim is the idea that the elections are perceived as less important than general elections, because they do not lead to government formation, or to the emergence of political leaders, and have little impact on public policy formation. Since there is less at stake than in national elections, turnout is

---

26. Figures cited in Nigel Bowles, *The Government and Politics of the United States* (London: Macmillan, 1993), p. 55.

27. In 1989 turnout in Northern Ireland, where a form of proportional representation is used for European elections, was 49.3% – compared with 36.2% in the rest of the United Kingdom.

## Table 3: Results by party and country – 1989

|  | B | DK | D | GR | E | F | IRL | I | L | NL | P | UK | Total |
|---|---|---|---|---|---|---|---|---|---|---|---|---|---|
| PES | 8 | 4 | 31 | 9 | 27 | 22 | 1 | 14 | 2 | 8 | 8 | 46* | 180 |
| EPP | 7 | 2 | 32 | 10 | 16 | 6 | 4 | 27 | 3 | 10 | 3 | 1 | 121 |
| ELDR | 4 | 3 | 4 | — | 6 | 13 | 2 | 3 | 1 | 4 | 9 | — | 49 |
| European Democratic Group | — | 2 | — | — | — | — | — | — | — | — | — | 32 | 34 |
| Greens | 3 | — | 8 | — | 1 | 8 | — | 7 | — | 2 | 1 | — | 30 |
| United European Left | — | 1 | — | 1 | 4 | — | — | 22 | — | — | — | — | 28 |
| European Democratic Alliance | — | — | — | 1 | — | 13 | 6 | — | — | — | — | — | 20 |
| Technical Right | 1 | — | 6 | — | — | 10 | — | — | — | — | — | — | 17 |
| Left Unity | — | — | — | 3 | — | 7 | 1 | — | — | — | 3 | — | 14 |
| Rainbow | 1 | 4 | — | — | 2 | 1 | 1 | 3 | — | — | — | 1 | 13 |
| Non-attached | — | — | — | — | 4 | 1 | — | 5 | — | 1 | — | 1 | 12 |
| Total | 24 | 16 | 81 | 24 | 60 | 81 | 15 | 81 | 6 | 25 | 24 | 81 | 518 |

*Includes one Social Democratic and Labour Party (SDLP) member from Northern Ireland.
Source: Info Memo 'Special Elections' No. 1 Revise Le PE Sortant et Listes de Candidats Actuellement Connues (Brussels: EP - Directorate of the Press, 22 March 1994).

lower and voters are much more likely to vote against the incumbents, often voting for small and new parties where they would not do so in general elections, perhaps from a sense that the elections represent a chance to protest without altering the government. What is not clear is whether large-scale protest voting resulted from a general protest about national politics or from an attempt by voters to find a way to express differing views on the European Community from those offered by the main parties.

Reif's analysis of the early European elections seems correct: the elections could be seen as second-order in terms of the campaigns and outcomes. In 1985 he even concluded:

> The Community subsystem of 1974 or 1979 or today, is politically clearly subordinate to its Member States. The European Community is a common subsystem of the ten Nation States. European elections are, thus, elections of members of a subordinate institution within a subordinate political system and their significance and nature has to be assessed as different from, say, elections to the national parliaments of the member countries.[28]

28. Karlheinz Reif (ed.), *Ten European Elections,* op. cit. (see above, note 6), pp. 1–2.

This analysis, appropriate in the early 1980s, seems to be less appropriate when applied to the 1994 elections. It is not self-evident that the EU is subordinate to the member states in the same way as it was, and within the EU system the EP's role has increased over the years. Whether these changes have had any effect on European elections is the theme of the following chapter.

# 3 EUROPEAN ELECTIONS 1994

Voters across Europe had their first opportunity to cast their votes as 'citizens of the Union' in June 1994.[29] This was more than a symbolic change: for the first time, citizens of one member state resident in another were permitted to vote in their country of residence. This change from previous European elections gave rise to the possibility, for example, of up to 50,000 British citizens resident in Spain voting there, while nationals of other EU member states living in Britain would be enfranchised in that country. While in the larger member states such changes were expected to have little impact on the elections and were relatively uncontroversial, they created considerable hostility in Belgium and Luxembourg, both of which have large numbers of resident European citizens. Luxembourg secured the right to insist that EU citizens must have been resident in Luxembourg for five years before they can vote in European elections.[30]

The introduction of European citizenship, the increased powers for the European Parliament and the controversy which had surrounded ratification of the Maastricht Treaty all seemed to offer reasons for greater participation

---

29. Article 8 of the Maastricht Treaty establishes citizenship of the Union. In addition to certain voting rights (Article 8b), Union citizenship allows citizens of one member state to gain protection by the consulate of another member state in a third country if their state does not have representation (Article 8c). Citizens may also move freely around the Union (Article 8a) and have the right to petition the European Parliament. Despite the limited nature of such citizenship, the very existence of legal European citizenship, pushed for by the Spanish, created anxiety in some states, notably in Denmark during the first referendum campaign in June 1992.

30. Article 8b also allows EU citizens resident in a member state other than their own to stand and vote in municipal elections. Here again special provisions have been made for Luxembourg, which will require EU nationals to be resident for ten years before acquiring these rights. EU nationals were not granted the right to vote or stand in *national* elections in other member states, as this was seen to cut too close to the heart of national sovereignty.

in 1994. The Maastricht debate had raised the profile of the EC, but had also ensured a burgeoning of anti-Maastricht groups in several countries — not just in those, such as Britain and Denmark, that were traditionally sceptical about European integration, but also in France, Germany and Portugal. While political leaders, especially in Germany, were still anxious to promote European integration, other opinion-formers, bankers, journalists and some politicians, as well as members of the general public, seemed less committed to the direction the European enterprise was taking.

If the debate over the Maastricht Treaty offered somewhat negative reasons for expecting the 1994 elections to offer more scope for debate than in the past, many of the provisions of the Treaty gave a positive reason for increased interest in the Parliament and the elections. Although the Treaty did not give the Parliament all of the reforms it had demanded in the Martin Reports,[31] it did grant the Parliament considerable new powers. An increase in the use of majority voting in the European Community pillar has brought with it enhanced powers for the European Parliament (set out more fully in Chapter 4).

The introduction of the right of parliamentary co-decision with the Council of Ministers in some policy areas, alongside the new provision for Parliament to give a vote of approval on the incoming Commission, meant that by 1994 the EP was being taken more seriously by politicians and members of the other European institutions. The old idea that the EP really did not matter, which had frequently served to explain low turnout in European elections, no longer held true.

In addition to the greater importance of the European Parliament, the increase in activities undertaken at the European level, notably within the two intergovernmental pillars created by the Maastricht Treaty to cover common foreign and security policy (CFSP) and justice and home affairs, gave a further reason for voters to be more interested in European affairs. However, despite all these factors, the elections differed little from previous European elections. Turnout continued to fall in most states, and the main focus of attention was again national. Only in France could a real shift be detected, with successes for Bernard Tapie's Energie Radicale and l'Autre Europe, the anti-Maastricht list of Philippe de Villiers, both of which secured

---

31. Prior to the Maastricht Treaty, David Martin produced three reports for the Institutional Affairs Committee dealing with Parliament's demands.

representation in the EP. The emergence of several small parties in Germany, particularly Manfred Brunner's Alliance of Free Citizens, did not result in electoral success.

This chapter assesses the campaigns and results of the 1994 elections. It looks at the transnational dimension in terms of the common manifestos put forward by the four transnational parties and party federations. Since the scope of transnational activity remained limited, the situation in each of the member states is then dealt with in somewhat more detail, before a final assessment of the trends in the results and their implications.

## Governmental agenda

The political background to the 1994 elections differed enormously from the situation five years earlier. In 1989 the Berlin Wall was still standing, the Soviet Union was intact, the Maastricht Treaty had yet to be written and most countries displayed positive attitudes towards the European Community, particularly in the run-up to 1992 and the internal market programme. By 1994, Germany had undergone unification and communism had collapsed across Eastern and Central Europe, paving the way for the re-emergence of many ethnic conflicts; the pattern of politics and security issues which had persisted during the Cold War had vanished and governments were forced to tackle many questions for the first time in forty years. In addition, long-term recession left politicians to face record levels of unemployment. Since all of these issues had repercussions at the European level, there was scope for some or all of the issues to be raised in the European elections, possibly serving further to interest voters, who had previously viewed the elections as remote and irrelevant to their daily lives.

Several issues on the governmental agenda in the twelve member states, often with long-term implications for the future development of the Union, could have been raised in the election. The most important of these were:

(1) *Enlargement* of the Union. Negotiations for the accession of the four applicant countries from the European Free Trade Association (EFTA) – Austria, Finland, Norway and Sweden – were completed in March 1994. All four states declared their intention to hold referenda before accession, allowing their citizens the opportunity to express an opinion about the future direction of their countries. Indeed, the Austrian referendum, which

overwhelmingly endorsed entry, was symbolically held on 12 June to coincide with the European elections. Enlargement does not only affect the acceding states, however. In particular, the more distant prospect of expansion of the Union to include the European Agreement countries (Poland, Hungary, the Czech and Slovak Republics, Bulgaria and Romania), Slovenia, and possibly the Baltics, Malta and Cyprus (Turkey being a more remote prospect), has considerable implications for citizens in the existing member states, ranging from the apparently minor fears of Scottish raspberry growers concerning imports from Poland to the anxieties of the Mediterranean countries which are currently the main recipients of cohesion and structural funds, and the likely collapse of the Common Agricultural Policy (CAP).[32] Yet voters in existing member states have never been asked their views on who should or should not be allowed to accede. The proximity of the elections to enlargement could have led to a debate on the future of the Union: wider *or* deeper, or wider *and* deeper?

Eftan enlargement also provided an ideal opportunity for *major institutional reform in the EU*, but such change did not take place. The Council of Ministers kept changes to a bare minimum, preferring to leave any major reforms for the 1996 intergovernmental conference, since there was little chance that agreement could be reached on the nature and scope of the reforms to be undertaken. Since many of the problems emerging from the Maastricht reforms have been attributed to a failure to consult the citizens of Europe, discussion of future reforms in the European elections would have been beneficial in overcoming similar alienation in 1996. As subsequent sections show, this approach was a rare phenomenon in the elections.

(2) *Unemployment was at record levels across the Union* (over 18 million and seeming unlikely to fall) and was increasingly seen as a problem that could best be tackled at a European rather than at a national level. Coming in the wake of Commission President Delors's White Paper on *Growth, Competitiveness and Employment*, European elections seemed to offer the opportunity for the issue to be raised and for parties of the left and right to propose their

---

32. The Spanish government's desire to keep the blocking majority at 23 out of 90 votes when qualified majority voting is in force, if three countries can rally 23 votes, or 27 otherwise, was partly explained by the question of the allocation of funds. The votes of the southern states of Spain, Greece and Italy just happen to equal 23.

strategies for tackling the problem. Thus, for the first time in European elections, there was scope for real discussion about a European problem based on left-right differences, with the possibility of taking into consideration the choice of free market economics versus interventionism as the best way forward for Europe.

(3) *Events in former Yugoslavia meant that for the first time since the end of the Second World War, the EC/EU had to face a clear military policy problem.* The situation highlighted huge differences in the attitudes of the member states in the field of foreign affairs. Attempts to create a common foreign and security policy as proposed in the Maastricht Treaty were still far from being fulfilled. There was therefore speculation that the lack of action in Bosnia, in particular, would lead to voters raising questions during the course of the European election campaigns.

(4) *Immigration* from the south and east, as well as the rise of Islamic fundamentalism in North Africa, is a serious cause for concern in several member states, helping the rise of parties of the extreme right, most notably the Front National in France and the Vlaams Blok in Belgium. While free movement of citizens under various European treaty provisions makes this a problem which needs to be taken seriously across the whole Union, there are large variations between countries in terms of how important they perceive these threats to be, making a pan-European approach difficult.

(5) *Economic and monetary union (EMU)* is a major feature of the Maastricht Treaty and one that has provoked great anxiety among citizens in many member states for a variety of reasons: in Germany there is a fear that EMU may lead to greater inflation; in Britain there is reluctance to lose a tangible symbol of national sovereignty, the pound sterling. The question has never been open to public discussion in most member states and the elections would have been an appropriate time to consider the issue.

(6) Increasing levels of international crime mean that the creation of *Europol* under the provisions of the third pillar of the Maastricht Treaty is a timely enterprise, potentially offering voters a concrete example of how 'Europe' is working for them. As is the case for defence, internal security is dealt with on a largely intergovernmental basis, with only a consultative role for the

EP. Nevertheless, discussion of work in this area could have helped overcome a certain amount of the secrecy which characterizes much decision-making at the European level and could have given voters a chance to see the relevance of the European Union in their daily lives.

Although politicians at both the national and the European levels were tackling these questions, to a large extent other factors determined whether any of them were put on the agenda in the European election campaigns. Thus, the national media had a significant impact on which issues achieved prominence in individual member states. Moreover, countries such as Italy and the Netherlands, which had recently held national elections, were still in the process of forming or consolidating their national governments and so there was minimal focus on European issues.

## The transnational manifestos

As on previous occasions, the transnational parties produced manifestos which their constituent parties could use as the basis for part or in some cases all of their campaigns.[33] In the preface to its manifesto, the PES noted that it was 'not a detailed programme, but rather a framework in which our future policies will be fleshed out'. Such a statement applied equally to the other parties as well: in general, the documents were rather bland and uncontentious, offering few substantive policies. Of course, this is not surprising when one considers that they are the product of negotiations between parties from numerous[34] countries working in several languages and that large national parties are themselves electoral coalitions shaped by national pressures. However, the situation does precious little to arouse public interest in the elections, or to give voters clear choices. Only the Green parties, fighting for the first time on a transnational manifesto, put forward a rather different approach to European integration, focusing on ecological as opposed to economic growth and fair trade rather than free trade.

33. The Party of European Socialists was the first to launch its manifesto, on 6 November 1993. It was followed by the ELDR Party manifesto launched on 10 December 1993 and the EPP manifesto on 25 February 1994 and the Green Parties on 22 March 1994.
34. The parties have members and associate members from non-EU countries.

The problems which surrounded Denmark's ratification of the Maastricht Treaty were reflected in both the ELDR and PES manifestos. The small Danish liberal party, Det Radikale Venstre, voted against the ELDR manifesto when other member parties rejected a proposed amendment that there should be some reference to the Edinburgh Conclusions in the manifesto.[35] The PES manifesto, on the other hand, included a footnote stating: 'This Manifesto must be read in light of the accords concluded at the European Council in Edinburgh in December 1992 that permitted Denmark not to be bound to certain areas foreseen in the Treaty on European Union.'[36]

*Unemployment* received much attention in the PES and ELDR manifestos. The PES argued that the problem had to be tackled by a coordinated European policy, suggesting a 35-hour or four-day week as possible solutions. Greater emphasis on economic and social cohesion was put forward as a way to help economic recovery right across the Union. Both the PES and the EPP manifestos advocated the implementation of the Social Charter, although the PES went further, laying out specific policies in the social field. The EPP stressed its support for a strong economy based on social market principles as the way to guarantee employment. The party put forward the view that cooperation between workers and employers was important in the implementation of policies to combat unemployment. ELDR support for the liberal market economy was reflected in its manifesto by demands for more flexible labour markets, albeit with the proviso that they should not come about at the expense of working conditions. The ELDR specifically called on the UK to abandon its opt-out from the Social Chapter.

Certain aspects of *environmental policy*, perhaps even more than unemployment, might best be tackled at a supranational level: global warming, acid rain and migratory birds are no respecters of national borders. The 1994 manifestos all took this into account. The EPP manifesto mentioned only the need for protection and cleaning up of the environment. The other parties were more specific, calling for a shift in tax burdens from labour to

---

35. The summary of the outcome of the European Council held in Edinburgh in December 1992, which clarifies Denmark's position in the Union.
36. This was the only footnote in the manifesto, a marked change from previous years when both the Danish Socialists and the British Labour Party opted out of large sections of the Socialist manifesto.

consumption and production. In the sphere of transport, the parties favoured a shift from road to rail or water transportation. The PES also called for a common European policy on waste, for an enforceable EU Environment Charter (although it did not indicate what this would entail) and for the implementation of the Rio Summit commitments.

In the field of *international security*, the three larger parties pledged their support to the numerous security institutions in Europe: the North Atlantic Treaty Organization (NATO), the Western European Union (WEU), the North Atlantic Cooperation Council (NACC) and the Conference on Security and Cooperation in Europe (CSCE).[37] The ELDR called for 'the establishment of a European security and defence policy with efficient military structures and forces to implement it'. Although recognizing the importance of NATO and the CSCE, the EPP asserted that the EU and its defence wing, WEU, must be able to operate independently if necessary. The PES, which is in favour of gradual disarmament, advocated the creation of 'a European peace-keeping force which will be made available to the CSCE and the United Nations'. The PES manifesto argued that once a common foreign and security policy was in place, the question of an EU seat on the UN Security Council could be addressed (but of course, no indication was given of how long this might take). Again reflecting a distinctive approach, the Greens called for the replacement of NATO and WEU by a 'pan-European collective security system'.

In its manifesto, the European People's Party pledged to fight 'exclusion, racism, xenophobia and discrimination', noting the importance of integrating people from other countries, not just those of the twelve EU states. The party expressed support for a common *immigration policy* for the whole EU (as did the PES), advocating aid as a way of preventing emigration from other countries. Although condemning racism, xenophobia and anti-Semitism, the PES acknowledged that the EU cannot unconditionally welcome everyone who would like to live there. It therefore advocated a policy which would give political refugees a right of asylum and victims of war or natural disasters a temporary right to stay, but which would look less favourably on people who wished to enter the Union for purely economic reasons. The ELDR manifesto recognized the need for common policies on immigration, noting the need for responsibilities to be shared, with member states bearing

---

37. The EPP manifesto did not explicitly mention the NACC.

the costs 'equitably'. The Greens were also anxious to uphold the rights of asylum seekers, viewing the EU as a possible arena for combating xenophobia.

All the parties expressed support for *enlargement of the Union* to the Eftan applicants and eventually the new democracies in East-Central Europe, but they also all emphasized that institutional reform must accompany enlargement.

In order to increase *democracy in the Union*, the EPP called for the drafting of a European constitution, based on 'subsidiarity, effectiveness and democracy'. It pointed out that there were certain matters which member states could no longer deal with effectively, suggesting that the Union should solve such problems, but noting also that this would require 'a reliable, balanced institutional system equipped with simple decision-making procedures and responsibilities'. In order to ensure democracy, the manifesto asserted, 'real supervisory and legislative powers must be vested in the European Parliament'. The ELDR called for the European Parliament to draw up a European constitution for a decentralized federal Union, and demanded the right of co-decision between Parliament and Council for *all* legislation, Treaty modification to be subject to Parliamentary assent, and legislative equality between the Council and the EP. The Greens also wanted a federal constitution to be drawn up, with movement towards a genuinely democratic European Union. The PES went further, demanding a right of legislative initiative for the Parliament and for 'co-decision between the European Parliament and the Council of Ministers and majority voting to be the rule'. However, the issue of increased accountability of the executive is not really tackled adequately in any of the manifestos.

Regarding *internal security*, the manifestos of the three larger parties all stated a desire for Europol to be established effectively as a way of fighting international crime, drug-trafficking and cross-border crime.

In summary, none of the manifestos made substantive proposals for a five-year legislative programme, nor did they even touch on the Community budget. They all mentioned the main issues currently being dealt with by national and European elites, but frequently in a platitudinous way rather than in terms of clear policy options. This was especially true of the four-page EPP manifesto and perhaps least so for the PES manifesto, which offered some clues as to how a Europe governed according to its principles might try to tackle, for example, unemployment.

Less attention was given to institutional reform and the need to increase the powers of the European Parliament than in previous manifestos. In the case of the PES this was partly the result of pressure from the British Labour party, which argued that institutional reform was not a vote winner and that it was, therefore, better to concentrate on unemployment and the environment. This seems to be a valid argument: domestic elections certainly tend not to focus on the minutiae of constitutional reform, nor on the detailed workings of legislatures; what matters is the impact the legislatures have on voters' lives. Because it is the Commission rather than the EP which proposes legislation, there is little point to putting forward a clear five-year programme when there is no guarantee that the Commission would take it up. Yet this means that it is difficult to convince voters of the relevance of European elections, either for them in their daily lives or for the future of the European Union.

Member parties of the transnational parties have a large degree of autonomy in the use they make of the transnational manifestos; they may supplement them with national manifestos or virtually ignore them entirely. Precisely how much attention is paid to the European issues outlined above is highly contingent on the practicalities of winning elections and on national political conditions. It is to these issues that we now turn.

## Countries

### Belgium[38]

Belgian citizens are Europe's most active participants in European elections, but only because voting is compulsory, with fines payable by non-voters. With little to separate the six main political parties (the Christian Democrats, Socialists and Liberals all have parties in both Flanders and Wallonia) on issues of European integration and a lacklustre campaign, the 1994 elections were particularly uninspiring.

Belgium's two Liberal parties portrayed the European elections as a test of strength of the governing parties prior to municipal elections due the following October. Despite high hopes arising from the apparent unpopularity of the Socialists and Christian Democrats in the wake of corruption scandals which had led to the resignation of three francophone Socialist ministers, the Liberals remained in second place in both Flanders and Wallonia, although they gained a seat in each of these two constituencies.

---

38. The countries are listed in alphabetical order according to the spelling in their own language.

## Belgium: European and national elections

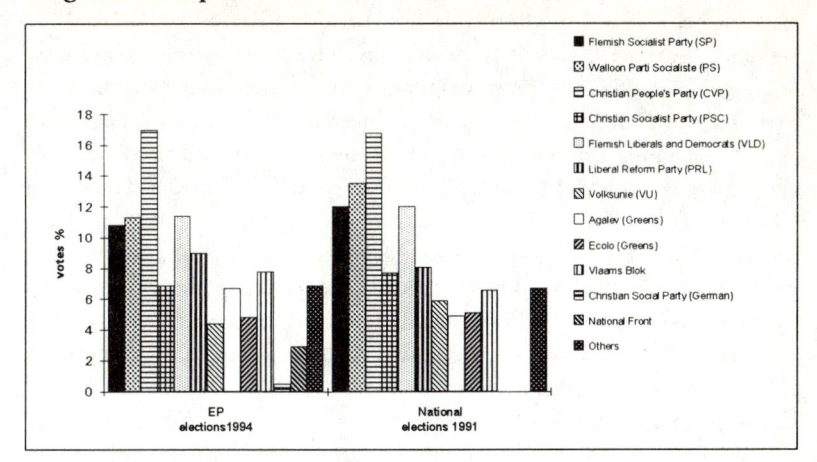

**Belgian seats in the European Parliament, 1994 (total = 25)**

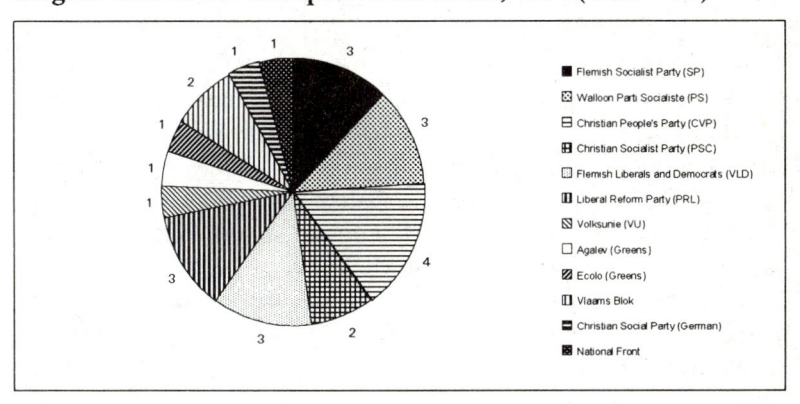

In the wake of the corruption scandals, the loss of two francophone Socialist seats was entirely in line with predictions. The small Flemish Volksunie party, which had been in danger of disappearing entirely, beat the predictions and returned one MEP to the EP, as in 1989. Like the governing Christian Democrats, it could feel comparatively pleased with the results.

An important change in attitudes towards European integration is occurring in Belgium. Traditionally very much in favour of integration, its people are displaying increasing hostility to any increased European activity in Brussels. Many of the half-million foreigners resident in Belgium are foreign civil servants, diplomats, senior businessmen and others located in Brussels because it is the home for NATO, the WEU Secretariat and the Benelux Secretariat, as well as for many EU institutions. This has recently led to anxieties about the proposed new voting rights in local elections. The issue is particularly sensitive in Flanders, since it is tied to linguistic questions.

The changing attitudes appear to have helped the parties of the far right: the Vlaams Blok gained an extra seat in Flanders and the National Front won its first seat in the francophone constituency.[39] Fighting on a racist platform similar to that of the French Front National, the Vlaams Blok played on the anxieties of citizens about the number of foreigners in Belgium. For the first time the party presented a bilingual manifesto and list in the Brussels constituency. A monolingual manifesto was produced in Flanders, however, since the party is essentially a Flemish party.

Nevertheless, these anti-European trends did not help the Greens, despite their calls for a reduction in the number of European institutions based in Brussels. In line with the trend away from the Greens right across the Union, the Green lists lost one of their three seats.

## Denmark

Voters in Denmark have had more opportunities than their fellow European citizens to express their views on European integration. Not only do the political groups which fight the European elections differ somewhat from the national political parties; the 1994 European elections gave voters their third chance in two years to vote on European matters, following the two referenda needed to ratify the Maastricht Treaty.

The Danes have never been the keenest participants in European elections, but turnout was an improvement on the 1989 levels, partly due to the large number of well-known candidates.[40] All the main parties with

---

39. Belgium was divided in four constituencies for the purposes of the 1994 European elections. There were Flemish- Walloon- and German-speaking constituencies; Brussels forms a separate constituency, with voters able to choose whether to elect MEPs from the Flemish or Francophone list. Fourteen seats were allocated to the Flemish list, ten to the francophone list and one to the German list. The Christian Democrat, Socialist and Liberal parties are all divided into French-speaking and Flemish parties.
40. Denmark's European election was held on Thursday 9 June but the votes were not counted until Monday 13 June in a cost-cutting measure decided by Poul Schlüter when he was Prime Minister. Thus any possible excitement the elections might have caused was lost.

## Denmark: European and national elections

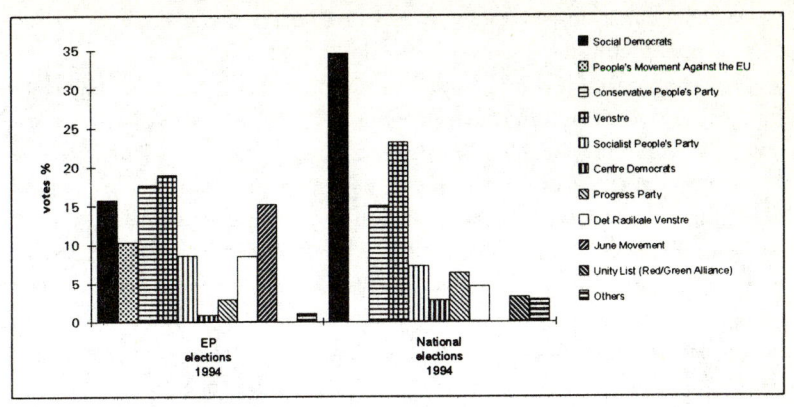

## Danish seats in the European Parliament, 1994 (total = 16)

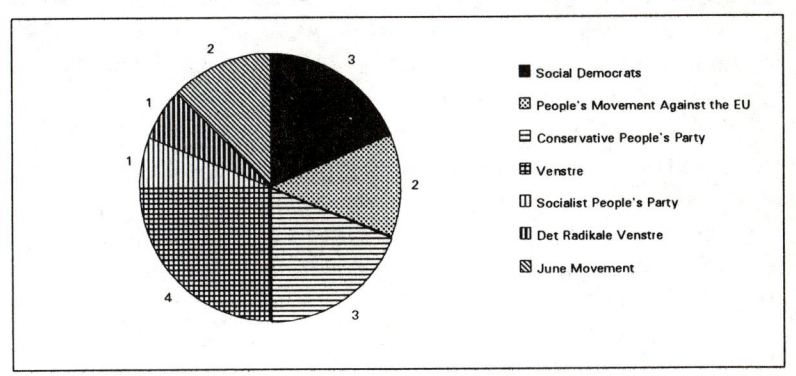

the exception of the Social Democrats fielded senior figures in 1994, leading to heavy use of preference votes in Denmark's flexible list system of proportional representation. Former Prime Minister Poul Schlüter headed the Conservative list, which gained an extra seat after fighting a somewhat Eurosceptic campaign. Schlüter's approach marked a distancing of the European policies of the Conservatives from the liberal party, Venstre. Venstre also gained a seat, but their success was the result of an improvement in domestic politics and the party actually performed less well than national opinion polls had predicted, partly because of the extremely pro-European attitude of its leader, Uffe Ellemann-Jensen. In an interesting twist the ruling Social Democrats lost a seat, while Lone Dybkjaer, the popular former Environment Minister, won a seat for the Radical Liberals.

The pattern for previous Danish European elections was essentially set by the 1972 entry referendum which gave rise to the People's Movement Against the EEC (later the People's Movement Against the EU). The People's Movement gave voters an anti-European option in European elections, which were thus not tied to national political issues. The June Movement was then set up after the 'No' vote in June 1992 as a more moderate anti-Maastricht party. The two groups gained over 25% of the vote between them, but failed to improve on the four seats won by the People's Movement in 1989.[41] Nevertheless, the strength of their support seems likely to provoke a cautious Danish position in the 1996 intergovernmental conference.

*Germany*
At the time of the 1989 European elections Germany was still divided and the citizens of former East Germany were not part of the European Community. After unification 18 observers were sent to the EP from the five eastern *Länder*. Thus the 1994 elections gave 12 million citizens in these *Länder* their first chance to vote for their representatives in the Parliament; but the elections were dominated by preparations for the federal elections which were due in October.

In the past, German political parties have strongly supported European integration and have advocated increasing the powers of the European Parliament far more vociferously than many of their colleagues from other national parliaments. The repercussions of the Maastricht Treaty seemed to have hit Germany, with members of the Christian Social Union (CSU) in Bavaria appearing to take a hard line on European issues and a former member of Commissioner Bangemann's cabinet, Manfred Brunner, fielding an anti-Maastricht list. Brunner's list failed to secure any seats, however, and the CSU's rhetoric seems to have stemmed from fears that the party might not reach the 5% *national* threshold in a larger Germany, rather than representing a real shift in policy.

There was little emphasis on European issues in Germany. This was partly due to the large number of elections (federal, state and local) in 1994 and from the relative lack of interest in European issues on the part of voters.

---

41. Had the two groups fought on a single list, they would have won five seats.

## Germany: European elections, 1994

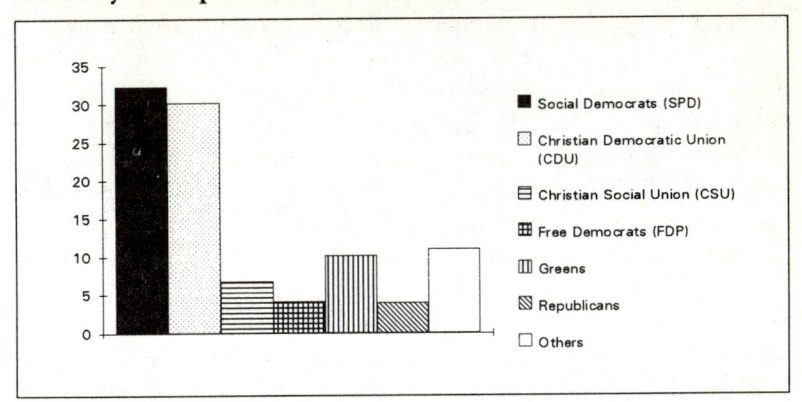

- Social Democrats (SPD)
- Christian Democratic Union (CDU)
- Christian Social Union (CSU)
- Free Democrats (FDP)
- Greens
- Republicans
- Others

## German seats in the European Parliament, 1994 (total = 99)

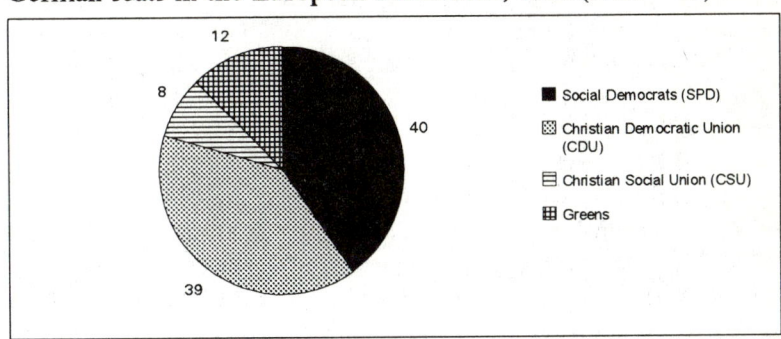

- SPD: 40
- CDU: 39
- CSU: 8
- Greens: 12

- Social Democrats (SPD)
- Christian Democratic Union (CDU)
- Christian Social Union (CSU)
- Greens

## Germany: national election, 1994

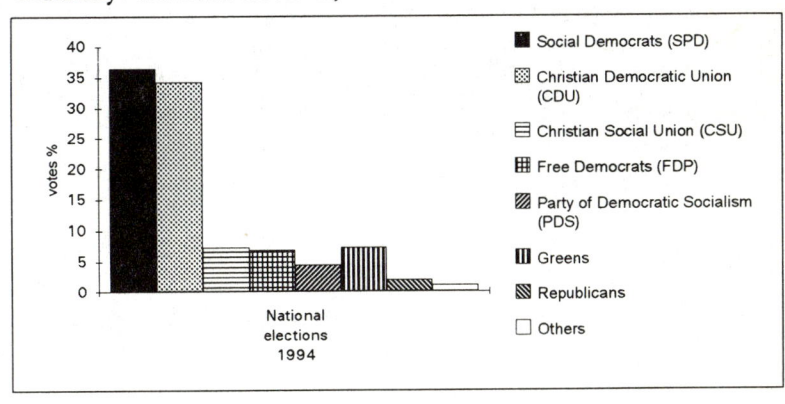

National elections 1994

- Social Democrats (SPD)
- Christian Democratic Union (CDU)
- Christian Social Union (CSU)
- Free Democrats (FDP)
- Party of Democratic Socialism (PDS)
- Greens
- Republicans
- Others

Although German parties may be the most enthusiastic proponents of further European integration and institutional reform, German citizens as a whole are not so committed. One clearly European issue that did little to increase waning support for the EU concerned European quotas on banana imports. Following new trade agreements there had been a reduction in the quantity of bananas imported from Latin America and a corresponding increase in imports from the African, Pacific and Caribbean states. This caused great discontent among the banana-loving Germans.

The outcome of the elections was affected by the change in the electorate to include former East Germany and by national considerations, with new anti-European parties achieving little success. The 5% national threshold was to prove a major hurdle for several parties in 1994. As in 1984, the Christian Democratic Union's (CDU's) coalition partner, the Free Democrats (FDP), failed to secure representation in the EP. These results, coming in the wake of a succession of poor results in state elections, seemed to bode ill for the federal election.[42] Similarly, the extreme-right Republikaner saw their support fall from 7.1% in 1989 to 3.9% and lost their six seats in the EP, a result which was viewed with pleasure by all the established parties.

The 4.7% won by the successor party to the former East German Communist Party, the Party of the Democratic Socialism (PDS), meant that it was also denied representation in Strasbourg. However, the strong showing of this party in the new *Länder* (with 40% of the vote in East Berlin) created some consternation among the established parties, not to mention leading to loss of support for the main opposition Social Democrats (SPD), who experienced their worst performance in European elections. The SPD had been hoping to perform well but was hindered by the PDS in the East and the Greens in the West, raising doubts as to its chances in the general election. Having first gained electoral success in the 1984 European elections, the Greens increased their representation from eight to twelve seats in the enlarged Parliament and, like the CDU/CSU and PDS, could view the outcome with pleasure.

---

42. Fears that were not realized: the FDP returned to the Bundestag in October 1994 with 47 seats.

*Greece*

In the past Greek elections, including European elections, have been treated somewhat like fiestas. This was not the case in 1994 when lacklustre campaigns were even deprived of the usual mass rallies by the two main parties. The elections occurred only eight months after a general election which saw the return to power of Andreas Papandreou and his socialist party, Pasok; the lack of enthusiasm was the result partly of voter fatigue and partly of a loss of support for Greek politicians. Voting is technically compulsory in Greece and the penalties for non-voting are high. However, sanctions are rarely imposed and this, coupled with the fact that registers frequently include people no longer resident in Greece, helps explain the low turnout of 71.2%.

The two largest Greek parties, Pasok and New Democracy, differ on European issues in tone rather than substance, so there was little scope for debate on European affairs in the elections. Only the Communists were opposed to Maastricht; the other parties favour further integration in the hope that a federal Europe may serve Greek interests well. This was the main thrust of an election which focused more on domestic than on European affairs. Unlike in the other eleven member states, however, attention to domestic problems in Greece includes the so-called 'Skopje problem', namely the presence on the northern border of the former Yugoslav Republic of Macedonia. The presentation, rejection and subsequent reinstatement of a Rainbow Party list composed of 21 candidates claiming to be Macedonians resident in Greece gave a certain resonance to the issue, on which the main parties held broadly similar views. Apart from the Skopje question the main excitement was a failed assassination attempt by extreme right-wingers against three members of the Communist KKE list.

New Democracy and Pasok both fared badly compared with their performance in the general election, but Pasok improved on its 1989 European election result (when the poll coincided with a general election victory for New Democracy) and gained an additional seat. Political Spring, the break-away right-wing party whose creation had led to the collapse of the New Democracy government in 1993, performed less well than expected, while the Centre Right Alliance (DIANA) narrowly failed to retain its seat in the EP owing to the introduction of a 3% threshold for the 1994 elections.

## Greece: European and national elections

*[Bar chart showing votes % for European elections 1994 and National elections 1993 with parties: Pasok, New Democracy, Communist Party of Greece (KKE), Left Alliance (SYN), Political Spring, Centre Right Alliance (DIANA), Others]*

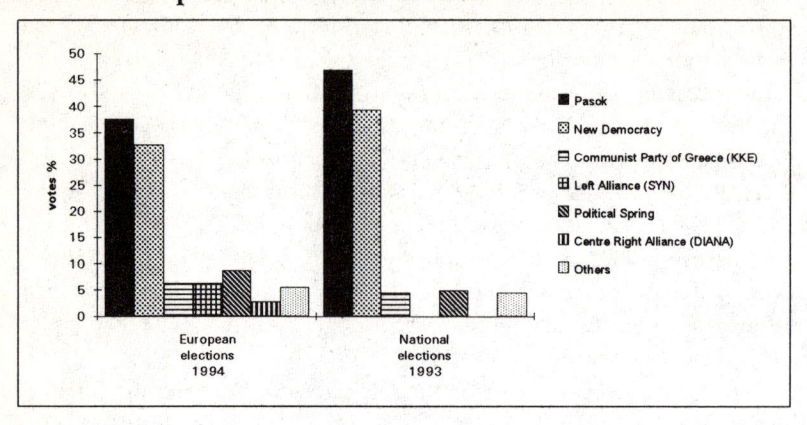

## Greek seats in the European Parliament, 1994 (total = 25)

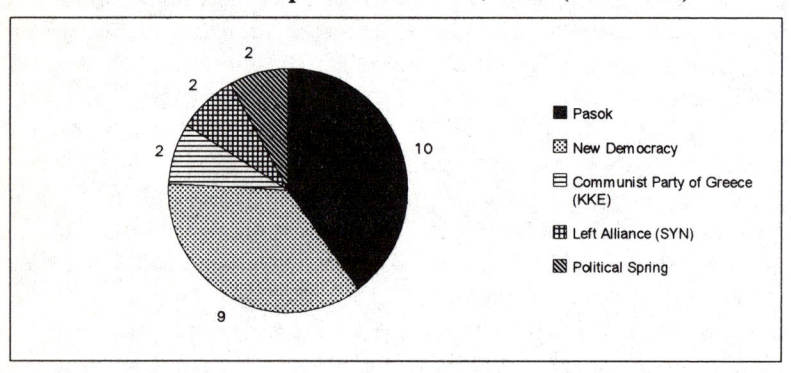

*[Pie chart: Pasok 10, New Democracy 9, Communist Party of Greece (KKE) 2, Left Alliance (SYN) 2, Political Spring 2]*

*Spain*

To listen to the campaign rhetoric of Prime Minister Felipe González, one might believe Spain still to have been in the 1980s, at the height of support for the European Union and its benefits for the then new Spanish democracy. The reality was very different. Not only had support for the European Union weakened in the face of prolonged recession, but the electoral supremacy of the Socialists finally came to an end. For the first time in post-Franco Spain the Partido Popular (PP) defeated the Socialists (PSOE) in a national poll. The PSOE owed its partial success in the 1993 general election to a personal vote for González and relied on Catalan

**Spain: European and national elections**

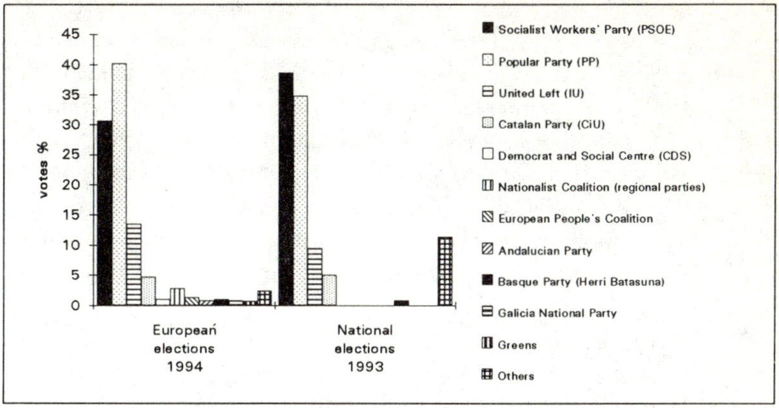
45
40
35
30
25
20
15
10
5
0
votes %
European elections 1994
National elections 1993
Socialist Workers' Party (PSOE)
Popular Party (PP)
United Left (IU)
Catalan Party (CiU)
Democrat and Social Centre (CDS)
Nationalist Coalition (regional parties)
European People's Coalition
Andalucian Party
Basque Party (Herri Batasuna)
Galicia National Party
Greens
Others

**Spanish seats in the European Parliament, 1994 (total = 64)**

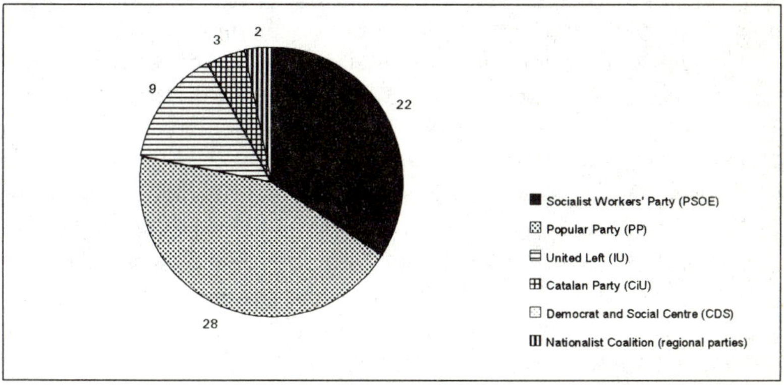
2
3
9
22
28
Socialist Workers' Party (PSOE)
Popular Party (PP)
United Left (IU)
Catalan Party (CiU)
Democrat and Social Centre (CDS)
Nationalist Coalition (regional parties)

nationalists (CiU) for support. In 1994, this support slumped further as the PP came first in 13 of the 17 provinces and the PSOE even lost its absolute majority in its former stronghold of Andalucia, where regional elections were held on the same day as the European election.

Unlike in 1989, when the Spanish economy was still strong, the rate of unemployment and the length of the recession meant that it was always going to be difficult for the Socialists to do well in 1994. However, the corruption scandals which hit the government in the run-up to the European elections contributed to the scale of the Socialist decline, as votes went to the PP and the far-left Izquierda Unida (IU). The CiU did not suffer from its association with the PSOE; indeed it actually gained a seat.

National issues featured strongly in the Spanish campaigns, partly as a strategic policy on the part of the PP, which is internally divided over questions of European integration. The PSOE fought the election on the transnational manifesto of the Party of European Socialists, while the PP used its own national manifesto. The PSOE tried unsuccessfully to argue that the elections were really about European, not Spanish, affairs, whereas the PP stressed the opportunity of inflicting defeat on the government. Attempts by the PSOE to resurrect the spectre of the far right failed to stop the haemorrhage of votes to the PP.

*France*

France enjoyed perhaps the most interesting European election, with a strange mixture of parties, alliances and personalities, reflecting both domestic and European considerations. The campaigns were not primarily about European affairs, but the presence of the 'Europe Starts at Sarajevo' list brought European foreign policy, or the lack of it, onto the agenda, and the anti-Maastricht lists of Jean-Pierre Chevènement on the left and Philippe de Villiers on the right were indicative of the hostility raised by the Maastricht Treaty.

With presidential elections due in May 1995, the parties of the right were anxious to build on their landslide victory in the 1993 elections and so the Gaullist Rally for the Republic (RPR) fought on a joint list with the Union for French Democracy (UDF). The apparent bargain was that the RPR would fight on the EPP manifesto, which the UDF supported in return for being allowed to field the right's candidate in the presidential elections. The reasoning was quite simple: the RPR's views on Europe were fairly evenly split, while the UDF did not actually have an obvious candidate for the presidency (apart of course from former President Valéry Giscard d'Estaing). The reality was far more complicated. Ratification of the Maastricht Treaty opened large divisions on the right and the list constructed had alternating RPR and UDF candidates. Dominique Baudis, the head of the list, was seen as pro-European and this may have partly explained the loss of support from Gaullist voters.

The ramifications of the Maastricht debate could be seen in the success of l'Autre Europe, the anti-Maastricht, anti-GATT party set up by Philippe

## France: European and national elections

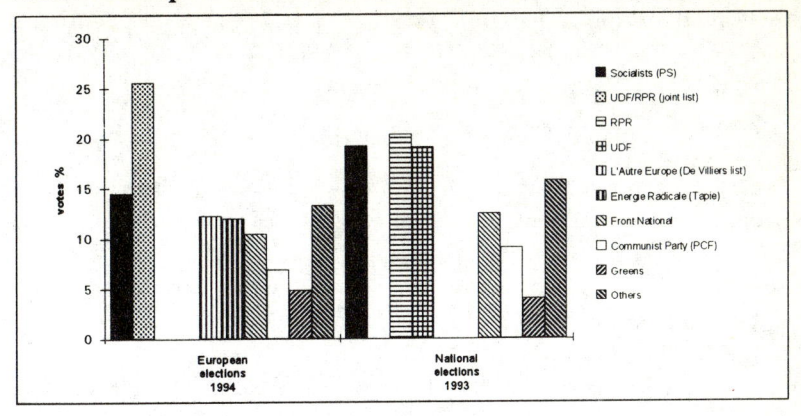

## French seats in the European Parliament, 1994 (total = 87)

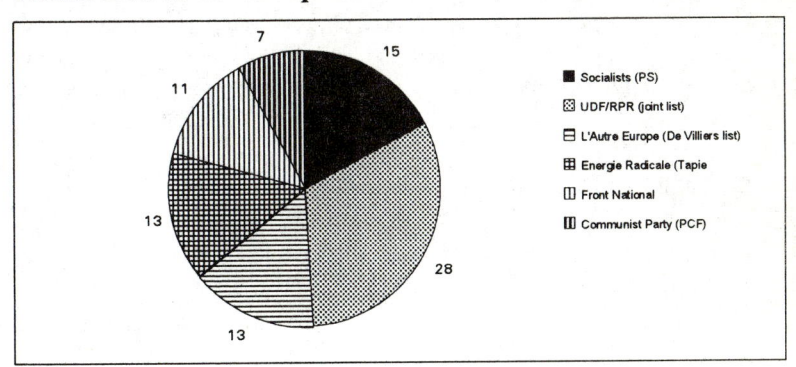

de Villiers and Sir James Goldsmith; it won 12% of the vote and 13 seats, many at the expense of the RPR/UDF list. However, Energie Radicale, the left-wing pro-European party led by the charismatic Bernard Tapie, also won 13 seats. Thus the elections did not demonstrate a clear move away from European integration, but certainly represented a threat to the established parties of all political colours.

Also in disarray following the European elections were the Socialists, who won only 14.5% of the votes and 15 seats. The party leader and presumptive presidential candidate Michel Rocard subsequently resigned. The Communist Party continued to decline, although it retained the seven seats it had held in the outgoing Parliament. Despite polling fewer votes than in 1989, the National Front picked up an extra seat in France's enlarged allocation. The Greens fell from their high point in 1989 and lost all nine seats.

*Ireland*
Irish voters and parties are broadly in favour of European integration — as major recipients of European money they are bound to be — and European elections do not excite much debate. There is, for example, general agreement that the MacSharry reforms of the Common Agricultural Policy were working quite well. The lack of interest was reflected in the drop in turnout to 44% from 68.3% in 1989.[43]

Nevertheless, the elections did create a fair amount of controversy in 1994. Ireland has traditionally had few successful women politicians. This time the leadership of Labour and Fianna Fáil both imposed female candidates who had only recently joined these parties on their Dublin constituency lists. The plan backfired and neither of these women candidates was elected, although three of the four MEPs elected in Dublin were women. Overall four women were elected out of Ireland's fifteen MEPs, compared with only one in the outgoing Parliament. Success for the two Green candidates (both women) contrasted with a relatively poor showing for the Greens across the Union and was seen largely as the result of widespread public concern about Sellafield (the nuclear processing plant on the Cumbrian coast).

Neither of the two governing parties, Fianna Fáil and Labour, performed as well as they had done in the 1992 general election, although both improved on their votes in the 1989 European elections, with Fianna Fáil gaining a seat. In a bizarre election in Munster the outgoing Progressive Democrat MEP, Pat Cox, resigned the party whip after the party's founder, Des O'Malley, was chosen to fight the seat. Cox fought and won the seat as an Independent.

---

43. The 1989 election coincided with a general election which helped boost turnout to 68.3%.

## Ireland: European and national elections

*Figure: Bar chart showing votes % for European elections 1994 and National elections 1992, with parties: Fianna Fail, Fine Gael, Labour, Greens, Independent, Progressive Democrats, Democratic Left, Others.*

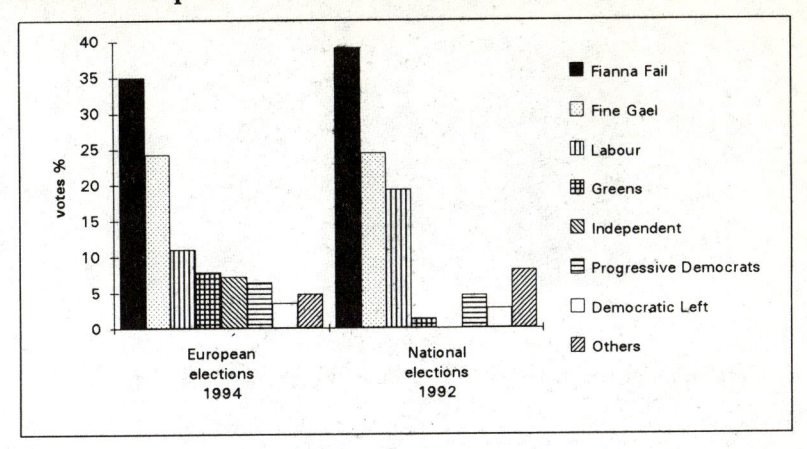

## Irish seats in the European Parliament, 1994 (total = 15)

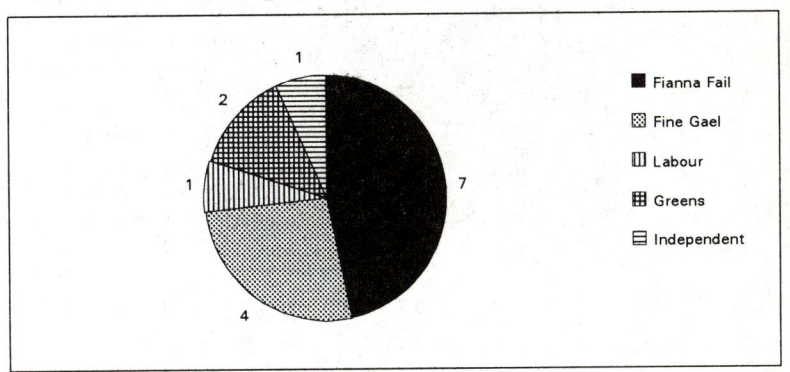

*Pie chart: Fianna Fail 7, Fine Gael 4, Labour 1, Greens 1, Independent 2.*

*Italy*

Coming less than three months after a general election which seemed to have fundamentally altered the shape of Italian politics, the European elections were overshadowed by domestic politics. The elections were the first to be fought by the Prime Minister's new party, Forza Italia, whose attitude to European integration was something of a mystery, and remained so after the elections.

The general election was fought under a hybrid electoral system under which three-quarters of the seats were chosen on a constituency vote and the

## Italy: National elections

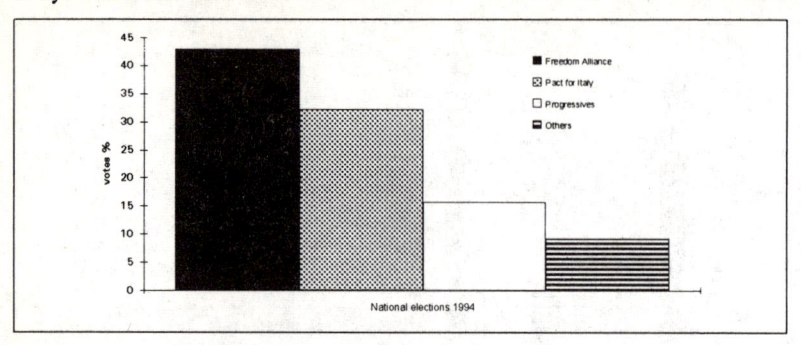

*Bar chart: National elections 1994*
- Freedom Alliance
- Pact for Italy
- Progressives
- Others

## Italian seats in the European Parliament, 1994 (total = 87)

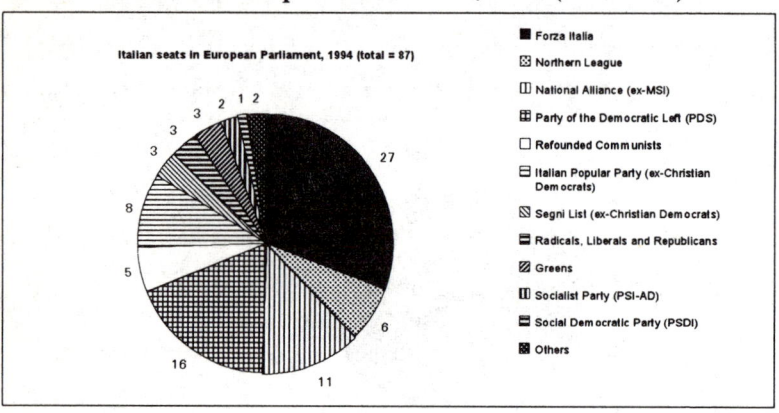

*Pie chart values: 27, 11, 16, 6, 5, 8, 3, 3, 2, 1, 2*

- Forza Italia
- Northern League
- National Alliance (ex-MSI)
- Party of the Democratic Left (PDS)
- Refounded Communists
- Italian Popular Party (ex-Christian Democrats)
- Segni List (ex-Christian Democrats)
- Radicals, Liberals and Republicans
- Greens
- Socialist Party (PSI-AD)
- Social Democratic Party (PSDI)
- Others

## Italy: European elections

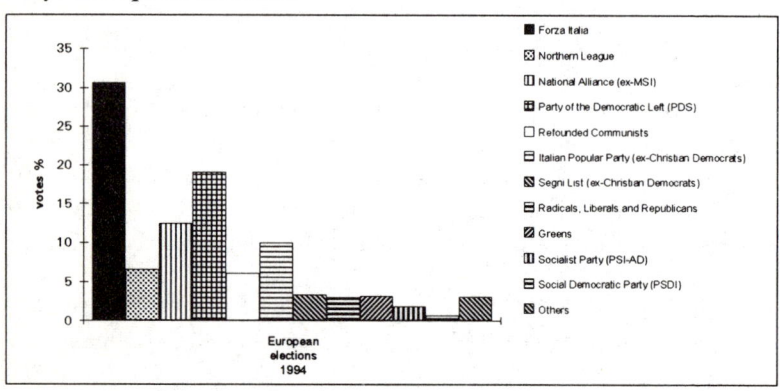

*Bar chart: European elections 1994*

- Forza Italia
- Northern League
- National Alliance (ex-MSI)
- Party of the Democratic Left (PDS)
- Refounded Communists
- Italian Popular Party (ex-Christian Democrats)
- Segni List (ex-Christian Democrats)
- Radicals, Liberals and Republicans
- Greens
- Socialist Party (PSI-AD)
- Social Democratic Party (PSDI)
- Others

remaining quarter on a proportional basis. This situation meant that Silvio Berlusconi had to form an alliance with the federalist Northern League led by Umberto Bossi and Gianfranco Fini's National Alliance, the successor party to the fascist MSI. The European elections were contested under the old proportional representation system with preference votes and thus enabled the parties to field individual lists.

Social Democrats, Christian Democrats and Liberals from the old regime were virtually wiped out as Berlusconi capitalized on his national popularity (not to mention his media enterprises) and Forza won 27 of Italy's 87 seats in the EP. The National Alliance also enjoyed strong support, winning eleven seats, but the third governing party, the Northern League, lost support to its allies. Of the old parties, only the former Communist Party, the Party of the Democratic Left (PDS), reached double figures (16 seats). Yet that was still a poor showing for the PDS whose leader, Achille Ochetto, resigned immediately after the elections.

The elections served primarily to consolidate the national position of Forza Italia, at least in the short term. They did little to indicate the government's stance on European affairs, although the Forza MEPs seemed to be a mixture of liberals and Christian Democrats, some of whom would have been at home in the EPP. There was speculation that Forza Italia might join the EPP group but in the event the party set up its own group, Forza Europa.[44]

*Luxembourg*

The President of the European Commission is not subject to direct election. However, on 12 June 1994, Jacques Santer went to the polls and was elected *twice:* once to the European Parliament and once as Prime Minister of Luxembourg. Luxembourg has a fixed five-year parliamentary term and since a general election was pending at about the time of the first European elections, it was decided for financial, administrative and symbolic reasons to hold the elections simultaneously, a practice which has been continued

---

44. The Rules of Procedure in force at the time of the election stated that to form a group with MEPs from only one country 26 members are required. Enlargement on 1 January 1995 led to a revision of the requirements and 29 members were thus necessary to form a group: Forza Italia had only 27 members and the group would then have ceased had it not managed to win over a member of the Northern League and one Social Democrat.

## Luxembourg: European and national elections

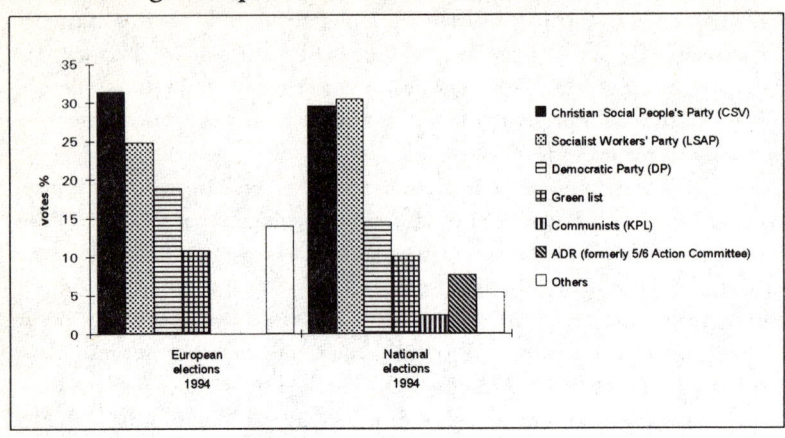

## Luxembourg's seats in the European Parliament, 1994 (total = 6)

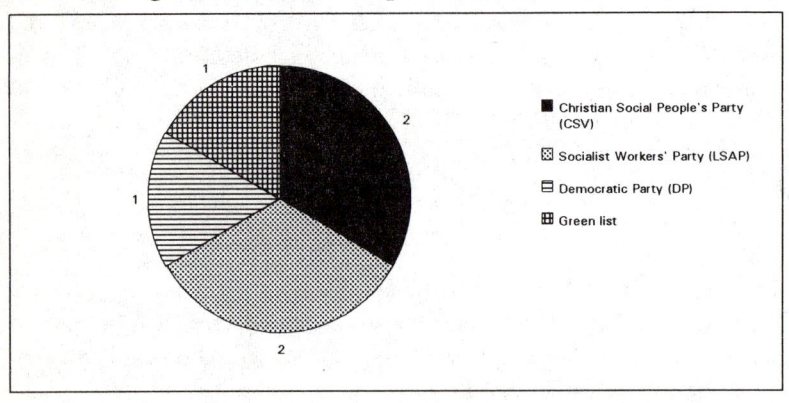

on subsequent occasions. This situation means that members of the outgoing administration can lead their party lists for both the national and the European elections, even though they resign their seats in the European Parliament on being reappointed to national government.

Coupled with the fact that voting is compulsory, simultaneous elections lead to a high turnout, but little focus on specifically European issues. However, the EU dimension necessarily forms a large part of the campaign since Luxembourg is so dependent on EU links, and parties stress their membership of transnational party federations, appending the European manifestos to national ones.

Despite the realization in Luxembourg that there is no alternative to membership of the European Union, traditional support for European integration has been tempered somewhat in recent years, as people are beginning to feel that there is excessive regulation from Brussels. The Single European Act is seen by many as detrimental to Luxembourg's economic interests, as it is now easier for foreign companies to locate there. Citizenship of the Union, especially in the sense of giving EU nationals resident elsewhere in the Union the right to vote in local elections, has further raised anxieties. Although the immediate problem of voting rights has been overcome, the issue has brought questions about Luxembourg identity to the surface.[45]

Three lists with candidates supporting nationalist policies were presented in 1994 but achieved little success. The winners were the Greens, who bucked the European trend and won their first seat in Luxembourg, reducing the Christian Democrats' (CSV's) representation to two. The Social Democrats (LSAP) retained their two seats and the Liberals their single one.

*Netherlands*

Dutch citizens have never been the most enthusiastic participants in European elections, but the 1994 turnout of 35.6% was low even by their standards. This was largely because the European poll took place only three months after local elections and barely a month after the general election. Thus voters were reluctant to turn out again following a short campaign overshadowed by the formation of a new cabinet, which was not finalized until mid-August.

However, low turnout seems also to stem from a belief among voters that the European Parliament still has little relevance to their lives, leading the press to claim that the EP and Dutch politicians should keep people better informed about what the EP can do. However, it is significant that voters appeared to be most interested in those issues such as foreign policy and justice and home affairs over which the European Parliament has least

---

45. Because foreign nationals make up approximately a third of Luxembourg residents, it has been agreed that they must be resident for five years before they will be entitled to vote.

## Netherlands: European and national elections

*Bar chart showing votes % for European elections 1994 and National elections 1994, by party: Christian Democrats (CDA), Labour Party (PvdA), Freedom and Democracy Party (VVD), Democrats 66 (D'66), Green (Rainbow list in 1984 and 1989), Coalition of Orthodox Protestants, General Association for the Elderly, Others.*

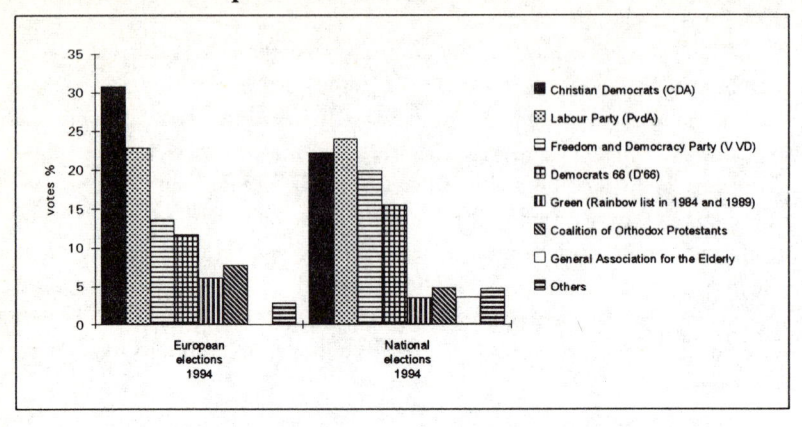

## Dutch seats in the European Parliament, 1994 (total = 31)

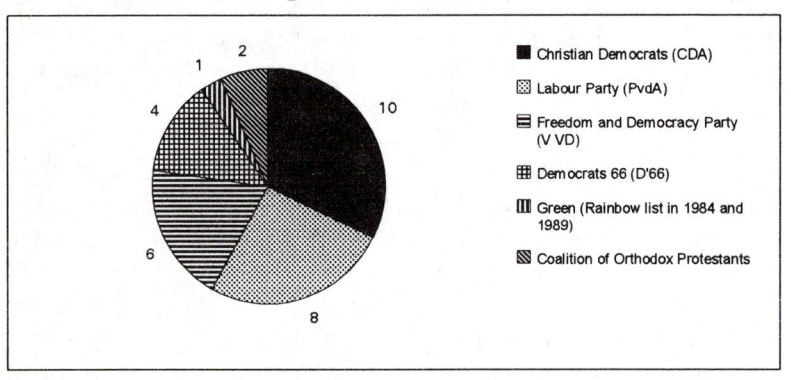

*Pie chart: CDA 10, PvdA 8, VVD 6, D'66 4, Green 1, Coalition of Orthodox Protestants 2.*

control, since they fall under the intergovernmental second and third pillars of the Union.

A shift away from support for further European integration also appears to have had an effect. Although the European elections received a fair amount of media attention, as in several other countries, this tended to be somewhat negative. There was little to choose between the largest parties, the Liberals (VVD), the Christian Democrats (CDA) and the Socialists (PvdA), in terms of their generally positive attitudes towards European integration. This led one commentator to call on voters hostile to further integration to stay at home, rather than vote for a pro-European party. While there were no explicitly anti-European parties, the two MEPs elected on the Dutch Reform Church lists joined the somewhat Eurosceptic *Europe des Nations* Group in the EP.

The results were similar to those in the general election, with the right-wing Liberals (VVD) and Democrats 66 (D'66) performing well at the expense of the Christian Democrats and Socialists. Since the Netherlands gained six new seats with the enlargement of the EP, the CDA and the PvdA did not lose any seats, but the other two parties each gained three. The Christian Democrats' result was better than in the general election because the General Association of the Elderly did not fight the European election and also because participation in European elections tends to be relatively greater among Christian Democrat voters in the Netherlands.[46]

*Portugal*
Falling between two bank holidays (Portugal Day on 10 June and the feast of St Antony on 13 June) the European elections failed to attract the voters away from the beach and turnout fell to 35.6%, putting Portugal alongside the Netherlands with the lowest figures in the Union. However, the bank holidays were only part of the problem: support for the European Union has weakened since the Maastricht Treaty negotiations, and there was a sense that the EP did not have much relevance to daily life; these sentiments, coupled with the late publication of lists and rather negative media coverage which focused largely on claims of MEPs' excesses, meant that there was little to inspire potential voters.

In line with the shift in public opinion, neither of the two largest parties, the ruling Social Democrats (PSD) and the main opposition Socialist Party (PS), fought an explicitly federalist campaign, although both are in favour of a single currency and the development of a common foreign and security policy. The Socialists criticized the PSD's use of structural funds and other resources, but otherwise there was little to distinguish the two parties.

Bringing an element of debate into the campaign, the Communist (PCP) and Christian Democrat Parties (CDS) vied for the 'Eurosceptic' vote. The

---

46. Comment by Sam Rozemond, cited in 'MEPs look for young voters', *Financial Times*, 3 June 1994.

## Portugal: European and national elections

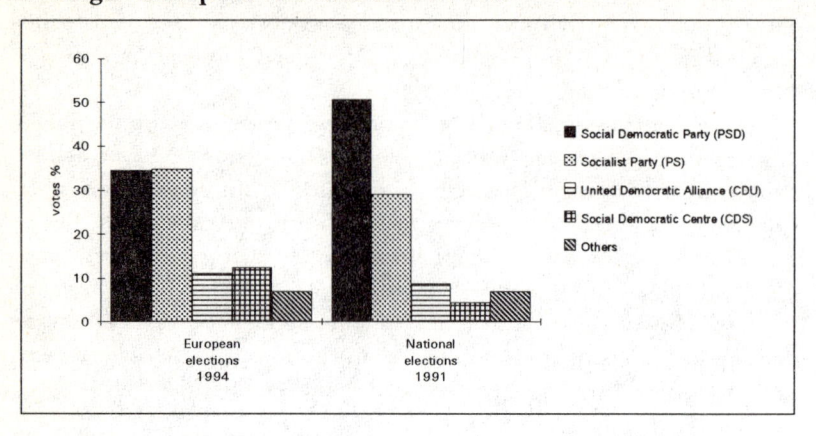

[Bar chart showing votes % for European elections 1994 and National elections 1991, with parties: Social Democratic Party (PSD), Socialist Party (PS), United Democratic Alliance (CDU), Social Democratic Centre (CDS), Others]

## Portuguese seats in the European Parliament, 1994 (total = 25)

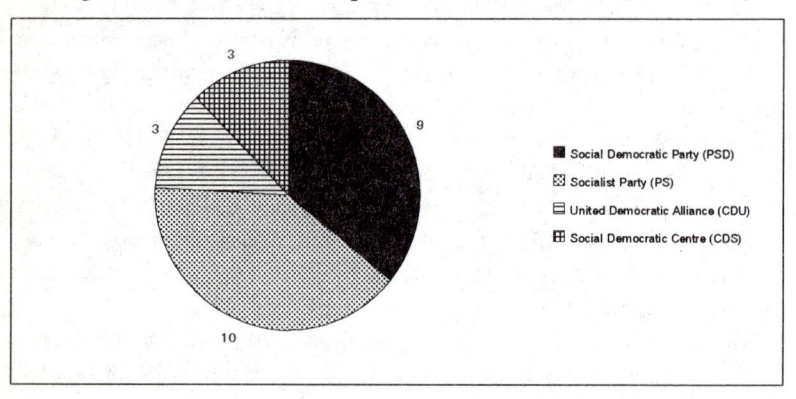

[Pie chart showing: PSD 9, PS 10, CDU 3, CDS 3 — Social Democratic Party (PSD), Socialist Party (PS), United Democratic Alliance (CDU), Social Democratic Centre (CDS)]

CDS performed marginally better than the PCP, which lost one seat. However, CDS support also fell, partly because Lucas Pires shifted allegiance and stood as an independent on the more pro-European PSD list.

The Socialist Party was the main winner in terms of seats, gaining two seats in Portugal's enlarged allocation of 25 seats.[47] Nevertheless it failed convincingly to defeat the PSD, whose support in percentage terms also rose by comparison with 1989. The outcome was therefore seen in a positive light by Prime Minister Cavaco Silva, who had expected a poor result in the light

47. Portugal had 24 seats until the 1994 election.

of a mid-term recession, in an election which was used more as a predictor for the general election due in October 1995 than as an expression of support for European MPs.

*United Kingdom*
The death of the Labour leader, John Smith, and the subsequent quest for his successor overshadowed the election campaign in Britain. Occurring just days before the scheduled launch of the party manifestos, Mr Smith's death meant a delay to the official campaigns, which stopped for a week at national level. Although activities at local level ceased only for a few days the impact had a significant dampening effect in elections which were never likely to gain much public interest. The Labour Party announced that there would be no campaigning for the party leadership until after election day. Nevertheless much media attention focused on the leadership issue, blurring the thrust of Labour's European campaign.

European issues have divided British political parties since long before the country's accession to the EEC in 1973. However, splits have been within rather than between parties and have rarely led to voters being offered clear choices on matters of European integration. In the past the Labour Party appeared more hostile to the EC, partly contributing to an internal division in 1981. By 1994, the party was committed to Europe and fought a pro-European campaign based on the manifesto of the Party of European Socialists. Despite this change in attitude, as in 1989, the party was anxious to use the elections as a mid-term referendum on the Conservative government and put little stress on European issues.

The Liberal Democrats were also keen to use the elections to attack the government and focused on domestic rather than European issues. As the only party which had consistently advocated a greater role for Britain in Europe, the Liberal Democrats were vulnerable to Conservative claims that they were the puppets of the EU. Thus the party toned down its message in the knowledge that its voters tend to be less enthusiastic about Europe than party activists. The strategy had only limited success since the Conservatives continued to portray the party as absurdly pro-European, an attack they also used on the Labour Party.

Having performed badly in the 1989 European elections when Margaret Thatcher waged a hostile European campaign, the Conservatives seemed set to fight a more positive battle in 1994. Yet the divisions which had previously beset the Labour Party put paid to this idea and the debate over the future of

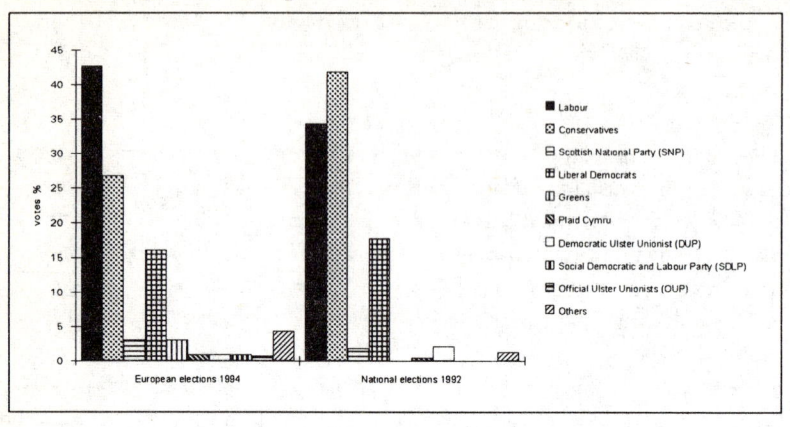

## United Kingdom: European and national elections

## UK seats in the European Parliament, 1994 (total = 87)

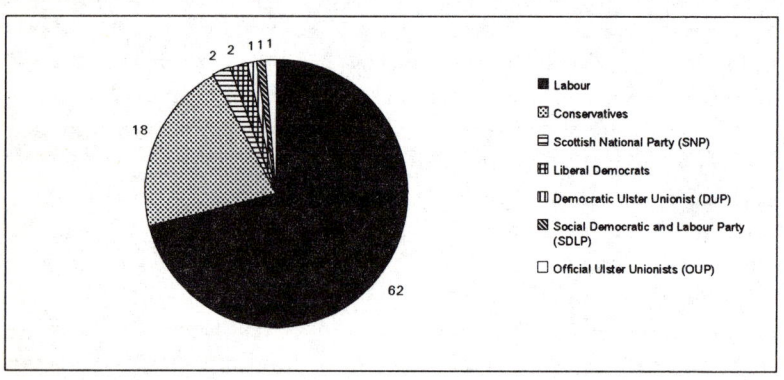

European integration took place largely within the Conservative Party. Aware of the difficulties which ratification of the Maastricht Treaty had raised for some of his backbenchers, the Prime Minister sought to appease them with proposals for a 'multi-speed, multi-tier' Europe and for flexible geometry.[48] Since he did not clarify what he meant by these terms John Major appeared, at least for a time, to have patched up divisions within his own party.

The Conservative approach seems to have been designed to win support from an electorate thought by the party to be increasingly hostile to the EU.

48. See *The Guardian*, 1 June 1994.

Whether or not that analysis was right, those voters who bothered to turn out voted overwhelmingly for the more pro-European parties. Although Labour has the British electoral system to thank for the fact that it is the largest single party in the EP, with 62 seats, it managed to win 44% of the votes on 9 June, with the Conservatives down to 28%. The latter could take only limited comfort from the fact that owing to very slim majorities their party succeeded in retaining 18 of the 32 seats it had in the outgoing Parliament; a further 2% swing would have left them with just 6 seats.

For the Liberal Democrats the elections were rather a disappointment, even though they won their first two seats since 1979.[49] The party gained only 17% of the vote and hopes of six or seven seats were unfulfilled (the loss of the Devon seat by a few hundred votes as the result of the presence of a *'Literal Democrat'* who obtained 10,000 votes came as a particular disappointment). The Scottish Nationalists were among the victors, claiming their second seat at the expense of Labour. The Greens, who had won 15% of the votes in 1989, declined as quickly as they had risen and secured only 3% of the vote. As in the past the three Northern Ireland seats went to two Ulster Unionists and one Social Democratic and Labour Party candidate.

## Summary

The 1994 elections, like previous European elections, focused primarily on domestic issues. Although there were exceptions to this, notably in France, Denmark and Germany, there was little sense of the elections being 'European', even where the campaigns extended beyond national politics.

There were few discernible trends in the results. Whereas the Greens performed well across the Community in 1989, there was no equivalent phenomenon in 1994. The most important aspect of the elections was therefore the increasingly fragmented state of European politics. Socialist parties performed slightly less well than in 1989, being left with 198 seats as compared with 197 in the outgoing parliament (in an enlarged EP).[50] This did not result in a Christian Democrat majority, but rather, as Chapter 4 demonstrates, in a parliament with several newly constructed party groups.

---

49. There were two Liberal MEPs in the indirectly elected Parliament when Britain joined the EC in 1973.
50. This was increased to 221 following the Eftan enlargement.

It was largely thanks to the vagaries of the British electoral system that the PES remained the biggest fraction in the EP. The European Parliamentary Labour Party (EPLP), with 62 members, is the largest component not only of the PES, but of the whole Parliament. This makes the group highly influential.[51] Its members chose to take the leadership of the EPLP, although they could have had the presidency of the Parliament; they hold the Chairs of the Environment and Social Affairs Committees. Variations in the electoral systems led to significant changes in the ELDR group as well. As in 1984, the German Free Democrats are not represented, but for the first time two British Liberal Democrats were elected.

As Table 4 shows, the elections rendered the EPP more fragmented than before, although less so than it might have been had Forza Italia joined the group, as was predicted at one stage. The creation of the 'Europe of the Nations' group means there is now for the first time a grouping in the Parliament whose *raison d'être* is to oppose further powers for the Parliament, but since it has only 19 members it is unlikely to prevent members from other groups pushing for further integration. The change to the Italian party system nationally means that of the three governing parties only the Northern League is in a major group (the ELDR). Similarly, the French presence in the larger EP groups has been reduced.

MEPs from France and Italy thus have a large influence within the groups of which they are the main constituent forces, but possibly less influence on parliamentary affairs as a whole than might otherwise have been the case. Conversely, Spanish MEPs do particularly well in the allocation of parliamentary jobs owing to the fact that, like the British and German MEPs, they represent only two major parties. This makes Spanish MEPs the second largest fraction in the EPP after the German Christian Democrats and the third largest in the PES, after the EPLP and the German Social Democrats; this has helped them to attain three vice-presidencies of the Parliament.

## Austria, Finland and Sweden – a note

The three new member states of the European Union have sent delegates from their national parliaments as Members of the European Parliament, pending European elections which they will hold in 1995/6. As was the case

---

51. Such a large delegation had made internal party discipline harder to maintain, however.

Table 4: Seats by party group and country – 19 July 1994

|              | B  | DK | D  | GR | E  | F  | IRL | I  | L | NL | P  | UK | Total |
|--------------|----|----|----|----|----|----|-----|----|---|----|----|----|-------|
| PES          | 6  | 3  | 40 | 10 | 22 | 15 | 1   | 18 | 2 | 8  | 10 | 63 | 198   |
| EPP          | 7  | 3  | 47 | 9  | 30 | 13 | 4   | 12 | 2 | 10 | 1  | 19 | 157   |
| ELDR         | 6  | 5  | —  | —  | 2  | 1  | 1   | 7  | 1 | 10 | 8  | 2  | 43    |
| United Left  | —  | —  | —  | 4  | 9  | 7  | —   | 5  | — | —  | 3  | —  | 28    |
| FE           | —  | —  | —  | —  | —  | —  | —   | 27 | — | —  | —  | —  | 27    |
| EDA          | —  | —  | —  | 2  | —  | 14 | 7   | —  | — | —  | 3  | —  | 26    |
| Greens       | 2  | 1  | 12 | —  | —  | —  | 2   | 4  | 1 | 1  | —  | —  | 23    |
| ERA          | 1  | —  | —  | —  | 1  | 13 | —   | 2  | — | —  | —  | 2  | 19    |
| EN           | —  | 4  | —  | —  | —  | 13 | —   | —  | — | 2  | —  | —  | 19    |
| Non-attached | 3  | —  | —  | —  | —  | 11 | —   | 12 | — | —  | —  | 1  | 27    |
| Total        | 25 | 16 | 99 | 25 | 64 | 87 | 15  | 87 | 6 | 31 | 25 | 87 | 567   |

Source: Info Memo 'Special Elections' No. 18 Session Constitutive – Le Nouveau PE au 19 Juillet 1994 (Brussels: EP – Directorate of the Press, 1994).

prior to direct elections, the composition of the different national delegations from the new member states has been determined by the results of the last general election.

Since the pattern of European elections has frequently been set by referenda on either accession or treaty revisions, a brief outline of the referenda campaigns and party attitudes in these three states may be helpful.

*Austria*

As a symbolic gesture, Austria held its referendum on 12 June, the same day as most of the European elections. Turnout, at 81.3%, was considerably higher than in the elections in the existing member states and the result – 66.4% voting for accession – gave the EU a positive sign. The outcome had been expected, but during the referendum campaign the decision of the popular leader of the Freedom Party, Jorg Haidar, to oppose entry led to fears that the result might be negative. The Socialist and Liberal parties were in favour of entry, as were the Conservatives, although the Conservatives had difficulty in retaining the support of their agricultural voters. Green supporters were opposed to entry, partly owing to fears about possible environmental damage caused by excessive transit of European lorries through the Tyrol and partly because of uncertainty about Austria's future defence role in the European Union. This was also a problem for the Social Democrats, who were reluctant to redefine Austrian neutrality. Advocates of entry felt that some compromise between neutrality

## Austria: national elections, October 1994

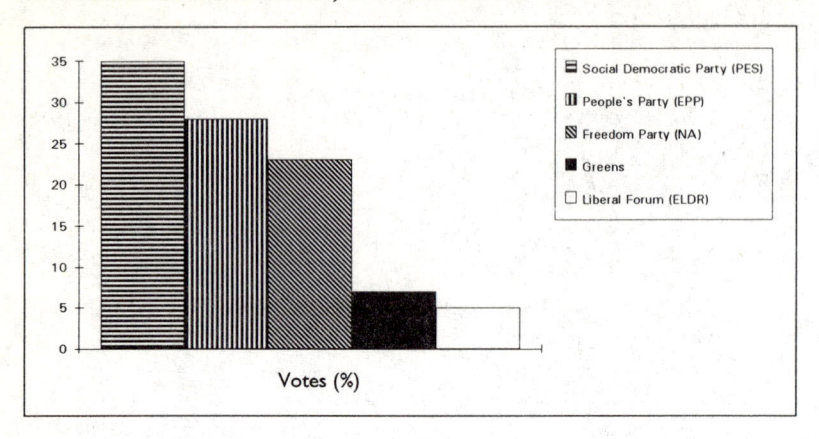

## Austrian seats in the European Parliament, 1995 (total = 21)

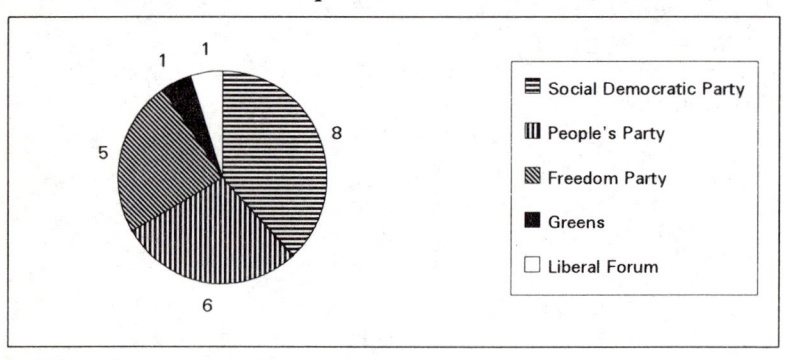

*Note*: Seats allocated on basis of votes in 1994 general election.

and membership of the West European Union might be possible, but the question was not settled prior to entry.

*Finland*
Finland was seen as the most likely of the Scandinavian applicants to decide to join and the outcome of the referendum on 16 October 1994 was a clear 'Yes', with 56.9% of the 74.2% turnout being in favour. Nevertheless the result was not inevitable and the governing Centre Party was split over the issue. (Two of the Centre Party's MEPs campaigned against entry, while the

## Finland: national elections, 1991

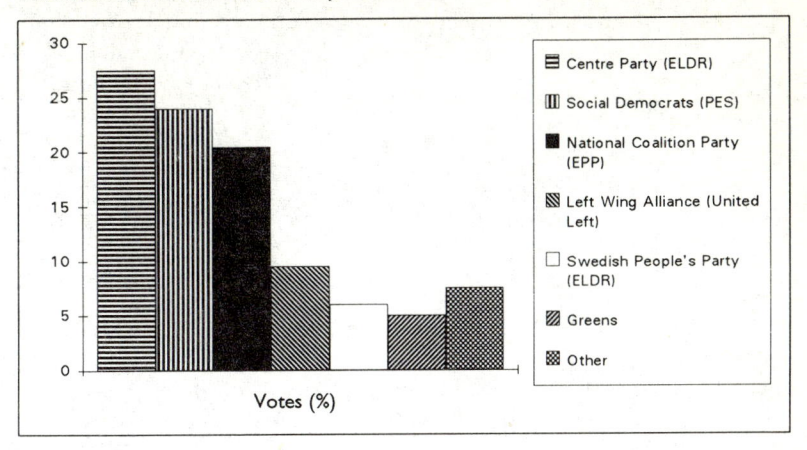

[Bar chart showing Votes (%) for: Centre Party (ELDR), Social Democrats (PES), National Coalition Party (EPP), Left Wing Alliance (United Left), Swedish People's Party (ELDR), Greens, Other]

## Finnish seats in the European Parliament, 1995 (total = 16)

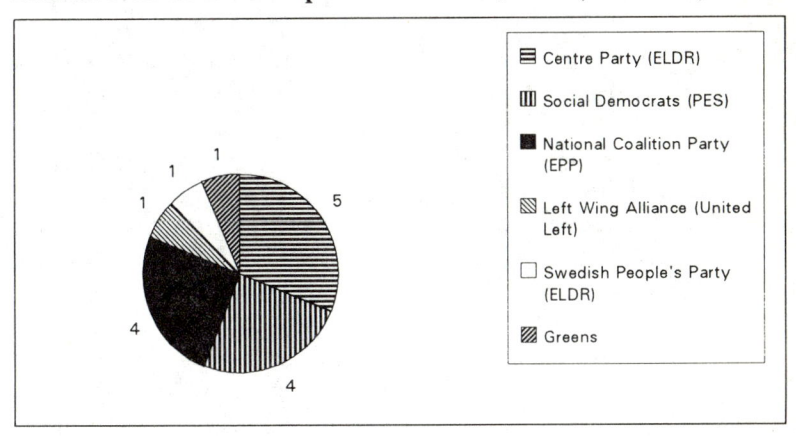

[Pie chart showing seats: Centre Party (ELDR) 5, Social Democrats (PES) 4, National Coalition Party (EPP) 4, Left Wing Alliance (United Left) 1, Swedish People's Party (ELDR) 1, Greens 1]

*Note*: Seats allocated on the basis of votes in 1991 general election.

other three were in favour.) The Social Democrats were split at rank-and-file level, but the leadership was strongly in favour; the Conservatives were the keenest advocates of entry. The Greens were also divided, although MPs were predominantly in favour. The Swedish People's Party supported entry, leaving only the Left Alliance clearly opposed. In general, electors in urban parts of Finland and in the south and west voted on general issues of military and economic security and tended to be in favour of entry. Those in northern and central Finland felt more personally affected by entry and many voted 'No' because of worries about adjustment for the food industries and for rural policy.

*Sweden*
Swedish entry to the EU was less predictable than that of Austria and Finland, but the referendum held on 13 November gave a clear 'Yes' vote: 52.3% on an 83.3% turnout.

Campaigners against entry argued that Sweden risked loss of sovereignty and suggested it would be better to wait until after the 1996 Intergovernmental Conference (IGC) to see just how much Sweden risked by joining; they also expressed anxiety about the implications of the EU's proposed common foreign and security policy for Swedish neutrality, and about possible reductions in Swedish environmental standards. Finally, they were opposed to the financial costs of entry. Advocates said that by acceding in 1995 they could influence the outcome of the IGC, that decisions taken on the CFSP area would be taken by unanimity and that the net costs would not be particularly great. Since adjustments to agricultural prices had already been made, the agricultural lobby was not as influential as elsewhere. In general there was support in industrial areas and from industrial unions but not from public-sector unions. The Moderate (Conservative) and Liberal parties were in favour, with the Social Democrats, Centre Party and Christian Democrats opposed, and the Green and Left Parties strongly opposed to entry.

EUROPEAN ELECTIONS 1994 § 59

## Swedish national elections, September 1994

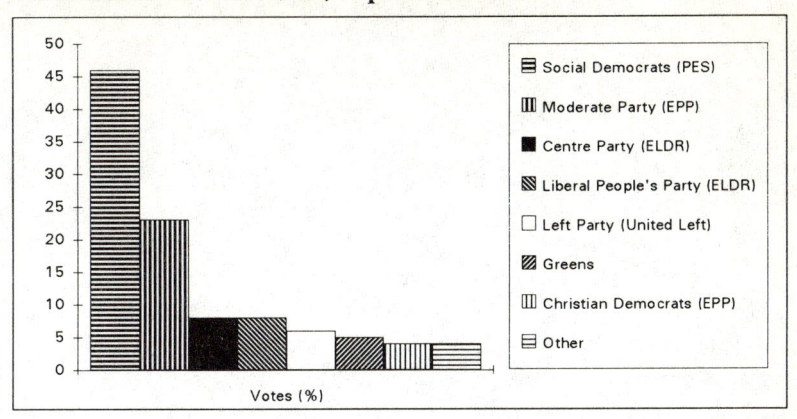

[Bar chart showing votes (%) for:
- Social Democrats (PES)
- Moderate Party (EPP)
- Centre Party (ELDR)
- Liberal People's Party (ELDR)
- Left Party (United Left)
- Greens
- Christian Democrats (EPP)
- Other]

## Swedish seats in the European Parliament, 1995 (total = 22)

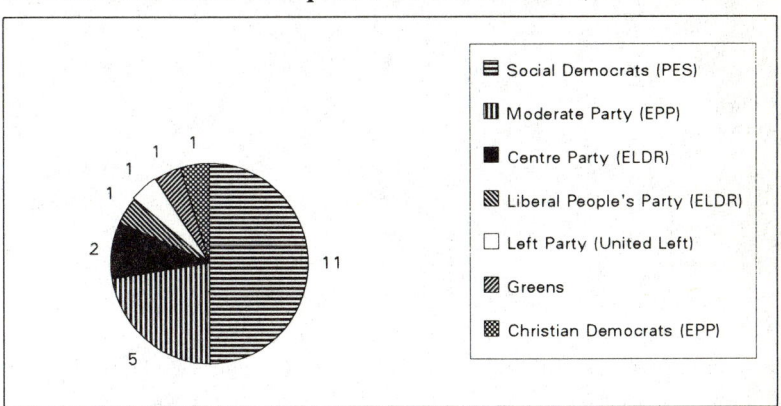

[Pie chart showing seats:
- Social Democrats (PES): 11
- Moderate Party (EPP): 5
- Centre Party (ELDR): 2
- Liberal People's Party (ELDR): 1
- Left Party (United Left): 1
- Greens: 1
- Christian Democrats (EPP): 1]

*Note*: Seats allocated on basis of votes in 1994 general election.

# 4 THE EUROPEAN PARLIAMENT

The European Parliament has become a key player in European decision-making. From being a consultative assembly composed of nominees from national parliaments, very much in the shadow of the Council of Ministers and the European Commission, it has become a directly elected co-legislator with the Council. Parliament's *treaty-based powers* have increased over the years, most clearly under the provisions of the Single European Act and the Maastricht Treaty.[52] The increase in the EP's powers arose partly from persistent lobbying by MEPs, but also in response to the need for scrutiny at the European level as more powers shifted from the national to the European level. As powers shifted, it is claimed, so the 'democratic deficit' in European decision-making increased. As it has become harder for national parliaments to hold ministers responsible for decisions taken in the Council of Ministers, MEPs argue that the EP should undertake a larger scrutinizing role, since it is the only body that can scrutinize the whole Council of Ministers.

Parliament has also become more *influential* over the years, with members of the Commission, and increasingly the Council, becoming much more willing to brief parliamentarians and to take their opinions seriously. The links between the Commission and the EP were further strengthened by the Maastricht Treaty. Article 158 provides for the Commission to be subject to a vote of approval in the European Parliament. In the past, the EP could dismiss the whole Commission but had no say over its composition; under the provisions of the Maastricht Treaty it now has a say in the appointment of the Commission as well. This new relationship not only makes the

---

52. The Single European Act, signed in 1986 and ratified in 1987, was the blueprint for the '1992' internal market programme. The principle of conciliation between the EP and the Council of Ministers was introduced in the SEA for non-budgetary matters (conciliation in the budgetary sphere had been introduced as early as 1975).

Commission more accountable to the Parliament, but is also felt by Commissioners and MEPs to increase the legitimacy of the Commission, frequently the target of much anti-European rhetoric.[53] By the time of the 1994 European elections, therefore, the Parliament was no longer the ineffective institution it had long been portrayed to be.

The aim of this chapter is to show how far the EP had evolved by 1994 and what impact the elections had, in terms both of composition and of the likely direction of the Parliament in the second half of the 1990s. The chapter begins with a brief summary of the history of the EP and an overview of how the Parliament works and the powers it possesses.

## The Common Assembly – a parliament in search of a role

The European Parliament began life in 1952 as the Common Assembly of the European Coal and Steel Community (ECSC). Accorded only supervisory powers by the Treaty of Paris (1951), the rationale for the Assembly was to give the ECSC some democratic credentials in the presence of the supranational High Authority, but it also served as a symbol for federalist hopes. Since the High Authority had been granted the right to act independently of the member states of the ECSC, the Common Assembly was created to oversee its activity. Although the Commissions which were created when the EEC and European Atomic Energy Community (Euratom) were set up by the Treaties of Rome (1957) did not have such powers to act independently, it was decided to maintain the parliamentary body. Whereas the three European Communities had separate Councils of Ministers and Commissions (or the High Authority in the case of the ECSC) until the 1965 Merger Treaty, the Assembly was simply expanded from 78 to 142 members to serve all three Communities. The Treaties of Rome extended the Assembly's powers in some policy areas from 'supervisory' to '*advisory* and supervisory'. There was little change in the Assembly's role, although since the Commissions had fewer powers than the High Authority, the Assembly's role was also somewhat reduced.

---

53. See, for example, reports of the hearings of Commissioners Oreja and Fischler, *Info Memo Special No. 8, Hearings of European Commissioners-Designate from Wednesday, 4 January to Tuesday, 10 January 1995* (Brussels: EP – Directorate of the Press, 11 January 1995).

Provision was made in each of the Treaties for direct elections of the EP but progress towards European elections, hampered by the crisis of the 'empty chair' and the Luxembourg compromise of 1965/6, was painfully slow. There was a problem that elections to a weak body were unlikely to attract voters and it was felt that low turnout would reduce the legitimacy such elections conferred on the Parliament. On the other hand, it was argued that the additional powers which might serve to interest the voters could not be granted to an unelected body. In the end the log-jam was broken by the introduction of direct elections, which followed an increase in Parliament's budgetary powers in 1970 and 1975. Such changes are typical of the incremental increase in the Parliament's powers, frequently arising because of a rise in general EU competences, rather than from a deliberate attempt to increase the EP's role as such.

The European Parliament of the 1990s has changed almost beyond recognition from the assembly of 1952 and is still evolving; MEPs make sure of that. Compared with other parliaments in Europe, the European Parliament is still relatively new and its members still feel it their duty as directly elected representatives of the citizens of Europe to push for further powers. This attitude transcends party boundaries within the EP since members from most party groups favour institutional reform of the European Union, including a larger role for the Parliament.[54]

Although it has acquired more powers, the EP remains significantly different from the national legislatures of *any* of the member states. European decision-making is a complex and lengthy business, with Parliament playing only a limited role. Following the various institutional changes which have occurred, it might be useful to consider the framework of EU institutions as more akin to the President/Congress relationship in the US than to the parliamentary democracies which typify western Europe. The powers conferred on the EP by the Treaties as amended by the SEA and the Treaty on European Union (TEU) offer certain parallels:

(1) MEPs have the right to confirm the executive in office via the vote of approval in the Commission, which, since the introduction of the

---

54. Although the *Europe des Nations* group created after the 1994 election does have a different approach to European integration and institutional reform, it is only a minor player in the European Parliament, leaving the EP's approach broadly unchanged from that of the outgoing parliament.

Maastricht Treaty provisions, has a five-year term of office running parallel to the EP's electoral cycle;
(2) the right of co-decision granted to the EP in certain policy areas gave it a limited right of veto;
(3) the EP has the right to reject the Community budget.

Having drawn this analogy, however, one must quickly enter several caveats: first, the institutional framework is far less clearly defined than that in the United States; second, many of the EP's powers are limited by the need to gain an absolute majority of members; third, the right of co-decision applies only in a limited number of areas (see Appendix 1); fourth, it must be remembered that the influence of the EP depends on relationships with the other institutions of the Union which originally tended to ignore it, although this has gradually changed over the years.

## Background information

### Seat allocation

The Common Assembly was enlarged from 78 to 142 members in 1958 when the EEC and Euratom were created. It subsequently increased to 198 members with the accession in 1973 of Denmark, Ireland and the UK. As the result of further enlargement to include Greece, Spain and Portugal in the 1980s, a revision of seat allocation which resulted from German unification and finally the accession on 1 January 1995 of Austria, Finland and Sweden, the EP currently has 626 members (see Table 5 for the breakdown of seats between countries).

The formula for dividing the seats, known as 'degressive proportionality', derives from a compromise reached when the Assembly was established. Although in principle the European Parliament represents the 'peoples' of Europe, with the Council of Ministers representing the states, to ensure that the smaller member states' interests are not entirely overridden in the European Parliament, this formula gives relatively more seats per head of population to small countries. For example, in 1994 there was one MEP per 610,000 voters in Germany, compared with one for every 38,000 electors in Luxembourg. Whilst such complicated arrangements have worked to date, with Luxembourg as the only tiny state, they contribute to the EU's reluctance to accept enlargement to include other tiny states such as Malta or Liechtenstein. As mentioned earlier, the Council of Ministers declared its

## Table 5: Distribution of seats

|  | 1995 | 1994 | 1989 | Population (millions, 1994) |
|---|---|---|---|---|
| Belgium | 25 | 25 | 24 | 10.1 |
| Denmark | 16 | 16 | 16 | 5.2 |
| Germany | 99 | 99 | 81 | 81.1 |
| Greece | 25 | 25 | 24 | 10.4 |
| Spain | 64 | 64 | 60 | 39.1 |
| France | 87 | 87 | 81 | 57.8 |
| Ireland | 15 | 15 | 15 | 3.6 |
| Italy | 87 | 87 | 81 | 57.0 |
| Luxembourg | 6 | 6 | 6 | 0.4 |
| Netherlands | 31 | 31 | 25 | 15.4 |
| Portugal | 25 | 25 | 24 | 9.9 |
| United Kingdom | 87 | 87 | 81 | 58.3 |
| Austria | 21 | — | — | 8.0 |
| Finland | 16 | — | — | 5.1 |
| Sweden | 22 | — | — | 8.8 |
| EC | 626 | 567 | 518 | 370.2 |

*Notes:*
1995: Enlargement to include Eftan states saw EP increase to 626 members.
1994: EP enlarged to take German unification into consideration.
*Source of population figures*: Info Memo 'Special Elections' No. 2 (Brussels: EP – Directorate of the Press, 10 February 1994); Austrian, Swedish and Finnish Embassies in London.

unwillingness to consider any fundamental reassessment of the composition of Union institutions before the Eftan enlargement because of the danger that existing compromises might come into question. Indeed, the relevant number of votes required to block a proposal in the Council of Ministers proved to be a source of contention in the final stages of negotiations for Eftan enlargement; it was possibly a foretaste of what could happen when more thoroughgoing reform of the institutions is undertaken.[55] Enlargement

---

55. The British, backed by the Spanish and Italians, were anxious that the 'blocking minority' necessary to prevent a decision when the Council acts on qualified majority should be kept at 23 in an enlarged Union. The intention of those countries was to make it relatively easier to block joint decisions and the row threatened to stall agreement on entry.

to the east will necessitate a more fundamental reassessment of the membership of the various EU institutions, including the rules for the allocation of seats in the European Parliament, probably entailing a reduction in the number of seats given to each member state, but with a greater emphasis on the size of population in each country.

*Composition of the Parliament*
MEPs sit in transnational party groups in the European Parliament (see Chart 2 and Tables 6 and 7). The groups are not fixed and can change at elections or even during the lifetime of the parliament. Although the bulk of the groups will remain the same over the course of the whole Parliament, odd members may join or leave during the five-year term. Such changes are most common in some of the smaller parties; for example, in the 1989–94 parliament, membership of the far-right Technical Group of the European Right frequently altered. Occasionally more significant changes take place. Thus, the European Democratic Group disappeared in April 1992, as British and Danish Conservatives followed their former colleagues, the Spanish Partido Popular, into the EPP Group. Similarly, when the former Italian Communist Party, the Party of the Democratic Left, joined the Socialist Group and the eight remaining members of the United Left Group joined the non-attached members, that group also vanished.

Membership requirements for groups are laid out in Parliament's own Rules of Procedure and were altered following the 1994 elections and again after enlargement in 1995. Thus to form a political group, there must be 29 members if they are all of one member state, 23 if from two member states, 18 if they are from three and 14 if they are from four or more member states.[56] Most of the groups do in fact comprise MEPs from several member states, although only the groups of the Party of European Socialists and the European People's Party have MEPs from *all* the member states. At the opposite end of the scale, Forza Europa was composed of members from a single *party*, Forza Italia, with 27 MEPs until enlargement forced the group to find two additional members from other Italian parties. Two other groups are predominantly French: the left-of-centre European Radical Alliance

---

56. See *Rules of Procedure* (Brussels: European Parliament, 8th edition, October 1993), Rule 29 on the formation of political groups and *Le Point de la Session, 16–20 janvier 1995* (PE186.904) for the revised membership figures.

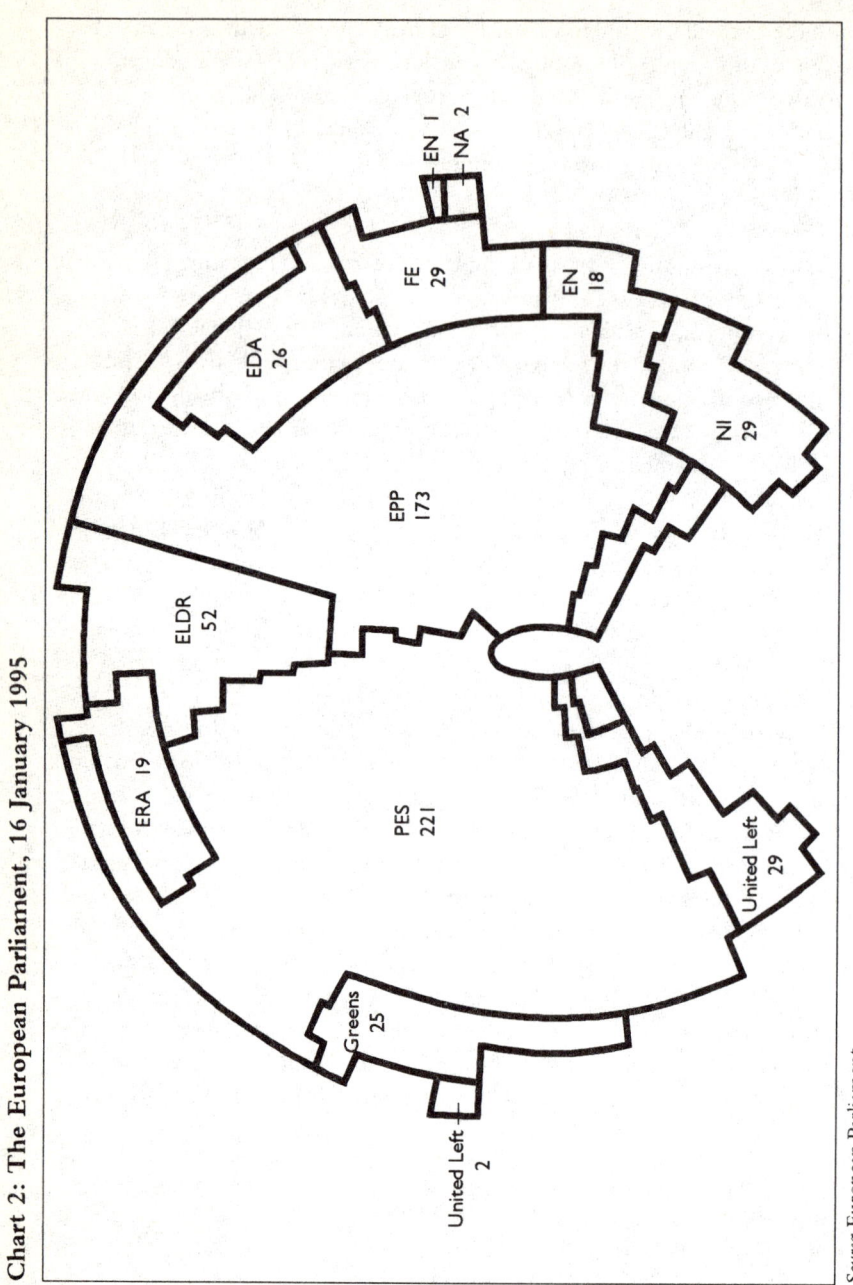

**Chart 2: The European Parliament, 16 January 1995**

- EN 1
- NA 2
- FE 29
- EN 18
- EDA 26
- NI 29
- EPP 173
- ELDR 52
- ERA 19
- PES 221
- United Left 29
- Greens 25
- United Left 2

*Source*: European Parliament.

## Table 6: Groups in the European Parliament

| Group[a] | Incoming 1989 | Outgoing 1994 | Incoming 1994 | January 1995 |
|---|---|---|---|---|
| Group of the Party of European Socialists (PES) | 180 | 197 | 198 | 221 |
| Group of the European People's Party (EPP) | 121 | 162 | 157 | 173 |
| European Liberal, Democrat and Reform Group (ELDR) | 49 | 44 | 43 | 52 |
| European Democratic Group (EDG)[b] | 34 | — | — | — |
| Green Group | 30 | 27 | 23 | 25 |
| Confederal Group of the United European Left[c] | 28 | — | 28 | 31 |
| Group of the European Democratic Alliance (EDA) | 20 | 20 | 26 | 26 |
| Forza Europa (FE) | — | — | 27 | 29 |
| Rainbow Group[d] | 13 | 16 | — | — |
| European Radical Alliance (ERA)[e] | — | — | 19 | 19 |
| Europe of the Nations (EN) | — | — | 19 | 19 |
| Technical Group of the European Right[f] | 17 | 12 | — | — |
| Left Unity | 14 | 13 | — | — |
| Non-attached | 12 | 27 | 27 | 31 |
| Total | 518 | 518 | 567 | 626 |

[a] Under Rule 29 of the EP's Rules of Procedure, MEPs may form political groups subject to the requirement that there are 29 members if they come from only one member state, 23 if they come from two member states, 18 from three member states, or 14 if they come from at least four member states. Provision is made for those who are not members of a party group to be non-attached.
[b] This group disappeared in April 1992, when the British and Danish Conservative MEPs joined the group of the EPP.
[c] This group disappeared in January 1993, when the Italian former Communists, the PDS, joined the PES. The group reformed after the 1994 election.
[d] This group ceased in July 1994.
[e] Created in July 1994
[f] Ceased in July 1994

*Source*: Compiled from data in *Info Memo 'Special Elections' No. 1 Revise* (Brussels: EP – Directorate of the Press, 22 March 1994); *Info Memo 'Special Elections' No. 18 Session Constitutive – Le Nouveau PE au Juillet 1994* (Brussels: EP – Directorate of the Press, 1994); *Info Memo 1* (Brussels: EP – Directorate of the Press, 4 January 1995).

Table 7: Composition of the European Parliament, January 1995

|  | B | DK | D | GR | E | F | IRL | I | L | NL | A | P | FIN | S | UK | Total |
|---|---|---|---|---|---|---|---|---|---|---|---|---|---|---|---|---|
| PES | 6 | 3 | 40 | 10 | 22 | 15 | 1 | 18 | 2 | 8 | 8 | 10 | 4 | 11 | 63 | 221 |
| EPP | 7 | 3 | 47 | 9 | 30 | 13 | 4 | 12 | 2 | 10 | 6 | 1 | 4 | 6 | 19 | 173 |
| ELDR | 6 | 5 | — | — | 2 | 1 | 1 | 6 | 1 | 10 | 1 | 8 | 6 | 3 | 2 | 52 |
| United Left | — | 1 | — | 4 | 9 | 7 | — | 5 | — | — | — | 3 | 1 | 1 | — | 31 |
| FE | — | — | — | — | — | — | — | 29 | — | — | — | — | — | — | — | 29 |
| EDA | — | — | — | 2 | — | 14 | 7 | — | — | — | — | 3 | — | — | — | 26 |
| Greens | 2 | — | 12 | — | — | — | 2 | 4 | 1 | 1 | 1 | — | 1 | 1 | — | 25 |
| ERA | 1 | — | — | — | 1 | 13 | — | 2 | — | — | — | — | — | — | 2 | 19 |
| EN | — | 4 | — | — | — | 13 | — | — | — | 2 | — | — | — | — | — | 19 |
| NA | 3 | — | — | — | — | 11 | — | 11 | — | — | 5 | — | — | — | 1 | 31 |
| TOTAL | 25 | 16 | 99 | 25 | 64 | 87 | 15 | 87 | 6 | 31 | 21 | 25 | 16 | 22 | 87 | 626 |

Source: *Info Memo* (Brussels: EP - Directorate of the Press, 4 January 1995).

(ERA), formed around 13 Energie Radicale MEPs; and the Europe of the Nations based on the de Villiers/Goldsmith party, l'Autre Europe.

A United Left group has reformed in the new Parliament, with members from the French, Greek, Italian (Refounded Communists, not the Party of the Democratic Left), Portuguese and Spanish Communist parties. The Group of the Technical European Right has ceased to exist, with members now in the non-attached group.

Members who are not part of any of the nine groups are described as 'non-attached'.[57] This entitles members to some of the privileges which are associated with group membership, particularly speaking time in plenary sessions and secretarial assistance. Similarly, the composition of the Committees is determined on the basis of group size. However, in all of these areas, there are benefits in being part of larger groups; for example, the method of allocating committee chairs and vice-chairs gives a *de facto* bonus to the larger groups, particularly the PES and EPP. This in part explains the decision of the British Conservatives finally to join the Group of the EPP: as members

---

57. The Ulster Unionist Ian Paisley and the French National Front members are among the non-attached members. In the 1989–94 Parliament the National Front members were part of the Group of the Technical Right; following the 1994 elections there were splits which led to the collapse of the grouping.

of the second largest grouping in the Parliament, they could hope for increased power and influence.[58]

*Official languages*
Following enlargement the European Parliament conducts business in 11 languages. This results in 110 different permutations for interpretation, compared with 72 previously.[59] Whereas the other EU institutions have English and French as working languages, representatives of the people cannot be required to have linguistic expertise (although in practice many do). This means huge costs are incurred in interpreting debates and committee meetings, the scope for fluent debate is reduced and the need for interpreters to take frequent breaks can limit the timings of committee meetings and constrains the scheduling of plenary and committee sessions. While it might appear sensible to reduce the number of languages that could be used in the Parliament, the issue is highly sensitive, with representatives of smaller member states determined to ensure the continued use of their own languages.[60] Thus it would be very difficult to introduce a ruling that certain languages could not be used. It might, however, be possible to create a solution whereby MEPs could speak in their native tongue but would only be able to receive interpretation in three or four languages. Such possibilities must be considered if the European Union is to enlarge further, not least because so many of the potential new entrants are small states, each of which would bring a new language to the Union.

58. Although whether the reality lived up to the expectations is not clear.
59. Although the introduction of additional languages creates more paperwork in translations, there are fewer problems than for interpretation since translations can be done via a third language, e.g. the Scandinavian languages are translated via English. This reduces the number of linguistic permutations which have to be tackled.
60. Just how sensitive an issue the linguistic question is was shown in the hearings of the Commissioners-designate in January 1995. Coming shortly after reports that French European Affairs Minister Alain Lamassoure felt the number of official languages should be cut to five – French, German, English, Italian and Spanish – Greek MEPs in particular were anxious to receive assurances to the contrary. In general the Commissioners-designate seemed to accept the necessity of preserving minority languages.

*Parliament's seat*

The European Parliament has three homes: Brussels, Strasbourg and Luxembourg.[61] This makes MEPs even more itinerant than would normally be the case for an MP and makes the EP less effective than it could be. Indeed there is suspicion on the part of some members that the decision taken by the Council to retain the status quo was in part a deliberate attempt to weaken the EP. Certainly the constant shuffling of people and papers between Brussels and Strasbourg does make it difficult for MEPs to keep a watch on the activities of the Council and the Commission. Admittedly, members of the Commission and Council attend plenary sessions in Strasbourg and answer questions there, but Parliament is still denied the easy access to officials from the other institutions that they have in Brussels.

Apart from the intrinsic problems associated with moving between two different places of work, the cost of the enterprise places a heavy burden on the EP's budget. Every month about a thousand MEPs, their assistants, interpreters and officials travel from Brussels to Strasbourg and back again. This alone is estimated to cost about 100m ecus (£75m) a year.

On top of this is the cost of the buildings themselves. The current situation was exacerbated by enlargement of the Parliament, which rendered the existing buildings too small. In 1993 a new parliament building with a chamber large enough to accommodate all members was opened in Brussels. This might have been expected to settle the question of the parliament's seat, since the Strasbourg parliament would be too small after enlargement. However, in 1992 the Council decided that Parliament should meet twelve times a year in Strasbourg. Many MEPs were hostile to this and there were mutterings that fewer than twelve sessions would be held in Strasbourg. However, even though only ten plenary sessions were held there in 1994, partly because of the European elections, twelve were scheduled for 1995.

Moreover, the President of the outgoing parliament, Egon Klepsch, signed a lease for a new building in Strasbourg. The decision was made following French threats not to pass the bill allowing enlargement of the Parliament to give Germany 18 additional seats in the 1994 elections, but it

---

61. The Edinburgh Summit failed to address the question in any fundamental way, preferring to institutionalize the status quo. In general plenary sessions take place in Strasbourg for one week every month, the other three weeks are spent in Brussels and the EP Secretariat and library are based in Luxembourg.

also partly reflects southern German preferences for Strasbourg.[62] This continuing situation means Parliament's standing in the eyes of the people is damaged since the whole process can easily be portrayed as a gravy train.

## How the European Parliament works

For British observers, the EP is a curious institution, lacking the theatre which surrounds Westminster. It is very much a scrutinizing rather than a debating chamber. In this it fits much more closely with the continental, particularly the German, parliamentary model, where the plenary is far less important than work done in committee.

Again peculiar from a British perspective, but less so for other countries, is the lack of a clear parliamentary majority. Much legislation requires an absolute majority of members (314 after the most recent enlargement), and because no group has a majority, members of the Socialist Group and the Group of the European People's Party frequently vote together to achieve the required majority.[63] No single group and no other grouping of parties can be relied on to give the required numbers. The results of the 1994 election did not significantly alter this situation.

The bulk of the EP's work is done in its committees in Brussels (see Appendix 3[64]) and by the time the plenary votes take place (usually in Strasbourg) the real problems of the legislation have already been ironed out.[65]

---

62. Additionally in the case of Klepsch the decision seems partly to do with a generational Franco-German affinity, not just the geographical preference of many German MEPs for Strasbourg.
63. Concerning the relationship of groups, see Rudi Arndt, 'The Political Groups in the European Parliament', *European Parliament 40th Anniversary Proceedings of the Symposium: The European Community in the Historical Context of its Parliament* (EP: Strasbourg, 1992).
64. As of January 1995, there were 20 Committees and a Temporary Committee on Inquiry, but the number of Committees and sub-Committees can change.
65. In an attempt to increase the efficiency of Parliament, its President, Klaus Hänsch, introduced a change to the old timetable for a trial period. Time was thus set aside for committee meetings on Monday evenings and Tuesday afternoons of the Strasbourg plenary sessions. The reasoning behind this revision was that any proposals referred back to committee by the plenary session could be dealt with immediately if the committees met during the Strasbourg week, and votes could be taken in the same session. In the past referral meant decisions could not be made for a month and the increased amount of activity arising from the new co-decision procedure made this situation unsatisfactory.

Thus debates in plenary are rarely of paramount importance and the rhetorical skills which can be so important for Westminster MPs hoping to make a name for themselves are of less use than the ability to chair meetings and undertake the technical scrutiny of EC legislation. Moreover, the opportunity to speak is controlled by the party groups, which are allocated speaking time strictly according to group size, and members who do not take an active part in committee procedures are unlikely to be called to speak.

Chairs of European Parliament committees can be influential. Just how influential they are depends on a combination of factors. The particular committee is significant: in areas where the Community has competence, committees and their Chairs can play a vital role – hence, for example, the increasing desire among MEPs to be on the Environment Committee. The ability of the Chair to push decisions through is another crucial factor, as are good links with members of the other institutions – members of Parliamentary committees can find out what the Council of Ministers and, especially, the Commission think on a particular issue and are likely to know fairly accurately whether amendments will be acceptable. Indeed this is one of the reasons why such a high proportion of parliamentary amendments (approximately 40%, taking first and second readings together) are successful.

Similarly, the rapporteurs chosen for different proposals can exert a much larger influence on European legislation than can backbenchers in Westminster. Although a rapporteur must gain the support of other members of his or her committee, and ultimately of the plenary, the right to draft the report in the first place is enormously important in terms of setting the agenda. Once a report has been drafted other MEPs may propose amendments, but the general tone will have been set by the rapporteur. Since the European Parliament's whipping system is very weak, rapporteurs must form majority positions within their own group on the committee and then a majority in the committee. Only then will the report or proposal be taken to the plenary. Once there, the debate is often attended only by members of the committee which has produced the report, since they are the only people who really understand the details. Other members come and vote in accordance with recommendations from their group leaders. Thus the opinions coming out of the committees can be virtually decisive.

In many cases, the role of the rapporteur is *reactive*, responding to Commission proposals and to the Council's common positions on such proposals. At other times, Parliament may decide to produce an 'own initiative report' in an area it does not feel has been adequately tackled by the other institutions. The use of 'own initiative reports' varies from committee to committee. They are particularly important in the Institutional Affairs Committee, which receives few formal proposals. Thus, the Martin Reports produced prior to the Maastricht IGC were drawn up to put the Parliament's position. A similar process will occur prior to the 1996 IGC, although this time the EP has a formal role, at least in the preparatory stages of the Conference.

It is through the work of its committees that the EP has begun to gain a reputation as a serious institution. At first, plenary sessions were often rather frivolous, with high rhetoric surrounding issues over which the Parliament had absolutely no jurisdiction. By contrast, the detailed scrutiny work of committees can be very useful, particularly when they have good Chairs and rapporteurs.

## The powers of the Parliament

A brief summary of the powers of the Parliament can give some indication of how important it now is in Community decision-making, but not what *sort* of an institution it is; the use those powers are put to and the way the Parliament interacts with the other EU institutions must also be considered. (The main areas of the EP's formal powers are laid out in Appendix 1; some key points of the rules of procedure, which indicate how Parliament intends to use those powers, are given in Appendix 2.[66]) A broader overview of the Parliament's powers including the changes which have come about over the years is given here.

Compared with national legislatures, the powers of the EP remain somewhat limited, although perhaps less so than is often assumed. Over the years the role of national legislatures has declined as powers have shifted to governments. This is true in the United States as well as in western Europe, but has been compounded in European Union states by processes of formal integration, contributing to the so-called 'democratic deficit' in European decision-making (outlined in the Introduction). Where decisions were previously taken by governments subject to scrutiny by nationally elected legislatures, or were actually taken by members of legislatures, increasingly

---

66. For a comprehensive view of the powers of the Parliament, see for example Jacobs, Corbett and Shackleton, op. cit. (above note 19).

decisions are made in the Council of Ministers which cannot be held effectively accountable to anyone, particularly when they are made by qualified majority. This problem is compounded by 'comitology', the situation whereby national civil servants vet Commission decisions implementing existing legislation without there being any provision for parliamentary scrutiny. As powers are being lost by national parliaments, the EP has gained some powers, but not enough to ensure adequate public accountability of decision-makers in the EU.

The powers of the European Parliament fit into four broad categories:

### 1. *Supervisory powers*

The Treaties of Paris and Rome all provide for supervisory powers. For example, Article 140 of the EEC Treaty provides that 'The Commission shall reply orally or in writing to questions put to it by the European Parliament or by its Members.'[67] The Council was not required to answer questions, but in practice it did so and this was formalized in the Stuttgart Declaration of 1983.[68]

The Treaties allow the EP to censure the Commission;[69] if the motion is carried by an absolute majority of members and two-thirds of votes cast, the Commission must resign *en bloc*. Since MEPs traditionally had no say in the composition of the incoming Commission, this seemingly important power is actually rather a blunt instrument, offering no scope for individual members of the Commission to be held to account. To date no Commission has ever had to resign. The existence of the power is useful, however; when the censure measure is threatened or tabled the Commission will try to avoid conflict.

Under the Maastricht Treaty the Parliament has gained more influence over the composition of the Commission via Article 158, which gives it the right to be consulted on the nomination for the Commission President and to vote on the incoming College of Commissioners. MEPs quickly demonstrated their desire to make use of this new right in the amended Rules of Procedure adopted in the Strasbourg plenary in September 1993.[70]

---

67. The Treaty of Paris did not specifically provide for questions.
68. Article 2.3.3 of the Solemn Declaration on European Union of 1983.
69. Article 24 of the ECSC Treaty, Article 144 of the EEC Treaty and Article 114 of the Euratom Treaty.

Although the Treaty only provides for Parliament to be *consulted* on the Presidency, Parliament decided to vote on the Commission President-designate following a declaration to Parliament.[71] Although this vote had no legal force, it was recognized by the potential candidates and the Council presidency that neither the individual candidate nor the Council would persist in a nomination that Parliament had rejected. Parliamentarians had their first chance to make use of this new procedure in July 1994. The Council's nominee, Jacques Santer, attended meetings of the PES, EPP and ELDR groups and answered questions, and then made a speech to the plenary session. Santer's nomination received muted support: 260 votes in favour, 238 against and 23 abstentions. The outcome was seen by many MEPs as demonstrating their willingness to challenge the Council. However, the result would have been very different had national considerations not prevailed. In general, the Socialists and Liberals were opposed to Santer, but the groups split in the vote largely because leaders of the governing Spanish and Greek Socialist parties and the Portuguese Social Democrats ordered their members to vote in favour. Thus the continued dominance of national politics prevented the EP making maximum use of its new powers.

MEPs also quickly announced their intention of conducting public hearings to assess the suitability for office of the Council's nominees for the Commission. Commissioner Pinhiero declared that this would be impractical and the outgoing President Delors advised against such action, but Santer himself accepted such arrangements.[72] In January 1995 Commissioners-designate were therefore each invited to appear before a parliamentary committee which would assess their competence and suitability to be Commissioners. Individual committees organized the hearings in slightly different ways, but in principle each candidate gave a short speech which was followed by two hours of questions designed to show general competence, attitudes towards the EP and towards questions of European integration, and knowledge of the proposed portfolio. Since the policy areas allocated to the various Commissioners do not overlap precisely with the various parliamentary committees it was decided that each candidate would be expected to

70. European Parliament 1993/4 Minutes of the sitting of Wednesday 15 September 1993. PE 174.510.
71. Rule 32(1) of the Rules of Procedure.
72. Reported in *The Guardian*, 16 August 1994.

attend only one hearing, organized by the committee most closely linked with their brief, but that other committees would also be able to send representatives entitled to ask questions. At the end of the hearings the chairman of the committee organizing the hearing asked the views of members in a closed session and then sent a letter to the President of Parliament, Klaus Hänsch, stating the general opinions of members regarding the candidate. The vote on the whole Commission took place ten days later and gave overwhelming endorsement to the Commission, with 416 votes in favour, 103 against and 59 abstentions.[73]

The right to vote on the whole Commission can be seen as an increase in parliamentary control of the Commission and may lead to closer EP/Commission links. Commissioners also stressed the increased legitimacy they felt it would give them. However, the experience in 1995 showed that the current provisions have serious flaws. MEPs expressed reservations about five nominees, but only three of these were criticized on grounds of competence and one of those was a question of the choice of portfolio, not general competence. The other two were criticized because of their apparent attitudes to the EP and EU decision-making. These reservations were not seen as giving sufficient grounds to reject the whole Commission, but had there been provision to vote on individual candidates, it is likely that at least one candidate would have been rejected. The desirability of collegiality in the Commission has been used to defend the requirement that Parliament vote on the whole Commission. However, the result is that the EP has a huge *de jure* power, which if anything is a disadvantage since it raises the Parliament's profile only to highlight the difficulty of using this power. There is thus significant scope for further refinements in this area of Parliament's powers.

Since European elections have tended to show a swing against governing parties in the member states, the vote on the Commission could potentially lead to inter-institutional conflict. Parliament and Council are often of different political persuasions: in 1994, most of the governing parties were of the right or centre-right, while there was a socialist plurality in the

---

73. MEPs were keen to point out, however, that a positive vote should not be construed as giving the Commission *carte blanche*. See *Strasbourg Notebook* (European Parliament, Directorate-General for Information and Public Relations, 18 January 1995).

European Parliament. If this were to result in Parliament pushing for a Commission reflecting its own political balance, tensions might also arise between the Council and the Commission. Such a situation was avoided in 1995, partly because nine out of twenty of the proposed College of Commissioners were socialists, thus making it unlikely that the Parliament would vote against the whole Commission.

*2. Budgetary powers*

The Parliament's gradual accumulation of power began in the budgetary sphere as the result not of any concerted attempt to increase its powers, but of the introduction of EC 'own resources'. In 1970 national contributions were replaced by 'own resources' composed largely of a percentage of VAT receipts across the Union and customs duties levied on third countries.[74] Since the EC now had funds over which there was no national control, it was deemed necessary to give the EP a role in this area. This led to the *Treaty amending Certain Budgetary Provisions of the Treaties* in 1970 and then in 1975 the *Treaty amending Certain Financial Provisions of the Treaties*. These two treaties ensured that MEPs played an important part in this Community activity. Although the powers were understood by only a handful of individuals directly involved in the budgetary procedure, they helped to gain the respect of the Commission, which gradually recognized the Parliament's importance. Indeed, members of the Budgets Committee are quick to assert the change in attitude which has come about. No longer can Commissioners summon MEPs to see them; if a Commissioner wants something from the Budgets Committee, he or she is expected to go to the Parliament, which can determine whether certain financial provisions are passed or not.

Each of the Community institutions drafts its own annual budget in February/March of the year prior to the one the proposals relate to and the Commission then prepares a preliminary draft budget in March.[75] Following informal consultation with Parliament, Council has a first reading in July and then in September forwards the draft budget to the EP, which has its first

---

74. In 1994 the EU's own resources came from the following sources: agricultural levies (2.9%), customs duties (18.0%), VAT (51.0%) and GNP resources (27.2%), with 0.7% miscellaneous. *Source: Report on the Budgetary Procedure, 1994 Financial Year* (Brussels: EP, DOC_EN\DV\248\248034, 1994).

75. Each institution leaves unchanged any provisions relating specifically to the internal budgets of the other institutions.

reading enabling it to propose amendments in October. After the plenary vote, the EP forwards its amendments to Council, which has its second reading in November. Again informal talks take place in an attempt to overcome any outstanding differences prior to the EP's own second reading in December. Council cannot reject second reading amendments that are passed by an absolute majority of MEPs and three-fifths of votes cast in the EP (providing total expenditure ceilings are not breached).

The 1975 Treaty permits the EP to reject the whole Community budget by a majority of current members and two-thirds of votes cast. MEPs availed themselves of this power in 1979 and 1984, rejecting the 1980 and 1985 budgets respectively, and in 1982 they rejected the supplementary budget, partly in order to demonstrate a willingness to use their powers in the aftermath of the first direct elections, which were seen to confer greater legitimacy on the Parliament. However, in general, Parliament prefers to act on specific budget lines rather than reject the whole budget; this enables MEPs to wield significant influence without resorting to the ultimate sanction of rejection.

In very broad terms, the Council has the last word on compulsory expenditure, i.e. spending arising 'necessarily' from the Treaties (largely, but not exclusively, spending related to the Common Agricultural Policy); the EP has the final say with respect to non-compulsory spending, as well as a veto on the whole budget. Changes in levels of expenditure are subject to a ceiling, 'the maximum rate of increase' calculated by the Commission on the basis of the trend in Gross National Product, average variation in the budgets of the member states and the cost of living trend.[76] Hence Parliament's room for manoeuvre is not vast.

The compulsory/non-compulsory distinction appears quite simple, but the reality is far more complex. In many cases the parameters of these types of expenditure are blurred. MEPs have begun to challenge the Council's classification of what constitutes compulsory spending; in the 1995 budget, Parliament acted on several agricultural budget lines which were theoretically 'compulsory' expenditure. The Council of Ministers has brought a case against the EP to the European Court of Justice as a result. The EP is not entirely unhappy with such a situation since it should help to clarify the situation in the future.

76. See *Memorandum to the Members of the Committee on the Budgets* (Brussels: EP, Doc_EN\DV\251\251401, 1 July 1994).

The *Interinstitutional Agreements* of 1988 and 1993, outlining 'financial perspectives' or guidelines for a five-year period, have further increased the budgetary powers of the EP, which now shares budgetary powers with the Council. While these agreements reduce the scope for the institutions to act on the annual budget, they do allow for greater control of the overall development of the budget and also aim to achieve a better balance between major items of expenditure. This proved to be somewhat controversial since the agreement did not take enlargement into consideration. In the 1995 budget procedure, therefore, Parliament successfully pressed for an increased ceiling to take account of Eftan enlargement.[77]

Parliament's role in the budgetary procedure also has implications for the legislative process, since MEPs attempt to bring as many proposals as possible under the financial provisions in order to maximize their influence on these issues. Additionally, MEPs now insist that where legislation has financial implications, Council should show that the necessary funds are available.[78] When this does not occur, Parliament may ask the Commission to revise the proposals; this gives it significant leverage over the other institutions. Moreover, MEPs may hold certain payments 'in reserve' pending agreement with the other institutions about their activities. In particular, in the 1995 budget Parliament withheld funds from so-called 'comitology' committees, i.e. management committees which deal with the implementation of certain legislation over which Parliament feels it should have some influence.

*3. Legislative powers*
The legislative process in the EC is complex, with at least eight different procedures.[79] Originally the Commission would propose legislation; the EP gave its opinions; and the Council had the final word on it. Changes in recent years have made matters more complicated, particularly since the introduction of the Single European Act and the Maastricht Treaty. In the past, the

---

77. The 1995 budget is 12% higher than the 1994 budget, but covers 15 countries instead of 12. For details see *The Week* (Strasbourg: EP, Directorate-General for Information and Public Relations, 12–16 December 1994, PE 182.856).
78. Article 7, para. 2 of the 1993 Interinstitutional Agreement.
79. Here a distinction must be drawn between the EC and the EU. The European *Union* comprises the intergovernmental pillars of justice and home affairs and defence, as well as the EC pillar, and the procedure mentioned refers only to legislation in the EC pillar.

EP had a largely *consultative* role with respect to some aspects of Community activity under the EEC Treaty. This was extended under the Maastricht Treaty to cover the new pillars of defence and justice and home affairs.[80] In addition, optional consultation has expanded over time.

The isoglucose judgment in 1980 was to prove extremely important for the EP's role in the legislative process.[81] The Court of Justice ruled that the Council was in contravention of Article 173 by failing to receive the opinion of the EP prior to taking its decision, and the act was declared void. This interpretation of the Treaty led the EP to change its Rules of Procedure in order to maximize its influence by delaying its opinions on Commission proposals if it is not satisfied with the response to its amendments.

The Single European Act increased the powers of the EP in certain areas, particularly those related to the internal market. The Parliament can maximize its powers by ensuring that as much legislation as possible is considered to fall under the internal market remit, where it has a significant role. The *cooperation procedure* which the SEA introduced (Article 149) is intricate, but basically provides for a second reading on legislation relating to the internal market, giving the EP more than just a consultative role in these areas.[82]

Under this procedure, the Commission proposes a piece of legislation which the Parliament and Council both consider. Parliament sends the proposal to the appropriate committee for consideration.[83] A rapporteur is appointed, who drafts a report, often with amendments. The rapporteur must then get the support of his or her committee, before presenting the report to the plenary debate in a first reading, at which point amendments

---

80. Article J.7 of the Maastricht Treaty states: 'The Presidency shall consult the European Parliament on the main aspects and the basic choices of the common foreign and security policy and shall ensure that the views of the European Parliament are duly taken into consideration. The European Parliament shall be kept regularly informed by the Presidency and the Commission of the development of the Union's foreign and security policy. The European Parliament may ask questions of the Council or make recommendations to it. It shall hold an annual debate on progress in implementing the common foreign and security policy'. Article K.6 makes similar provisions for the justice and home affairs pillar of the Union.
81. Isoglucose judgment of 29 October 1980 of the Court of Justice of the European Communities, cases 137/79 and 138/79.
82. Article 7 of the SEA.
83. In some cases the proposal is considered in more than one committee, but only one will be charged with the task of producing a report.

may be agreed. Since proposals are complicated, it is frequently only members of the relevant committees who understand them and attend the plenary sessions; other MEPs come and vote according to the recommendation of the leader of their group.

Following Parliament's first reading, Council announces its 'common position' (for which a qualified majority is sufficient). The proposal is then returned to the EP and considered by the same committee which considered it at first reading. The scope of EP action at this stage is rather limited since, according to its own Rules of Procedure, the EP can only table 'amendments which would restore Parliament's first reading in whole or in part' or represent a compromise; such amendments require an absolute majority normally of 314 votes (260 until June 1994).

Parliamentary power arises from the existence of the second Council reading. If the Commission has accepted the EP's amendments to the common position, the Council can pass the amended proposal by a qualified majority. The Council can accept only by unanimity any parliamentary amendments not accepted by the Commission. If the EP has rejected the common position, the Council can again adopt it only by unanimity. This procedure strengthens the position of the EP since it only requires one ally on the Council to ensure the rejection of a proposal if the Commission does not accept the amendments. Thus, the Commission is more likely to accept parliamentary amendments rather than risk losing the measure entirely, since it is generally anxious to ensure that legislation which has reached this stage should get through.[84] An early example of the potential scope for parliamentary action was given in the case of small car emissions outlined in Box 2.[85] Since the Council of Ministers was divided over the details, the EP managed

---

84. For a further analysis of the cooperation procedure see, for example, Vernon Bogdanor, 'The June 1989 European Elections and the Institutions of the Community', *Government and Opposition*, vol. 24, 1989, pp. 199–214; Richard Corbett, 'Testing the New Procedures: The European Parliament's First Experiences with its New "Single Act" Powers', *JCMS*, vol. 27, no. 4, June 1989, pp. 359–72; John Fitzmaurice, 'An Analysis of the European Community's Co-operation Procedure' *JCMS*, vol. 26, no. 4, June 1988, pp. 389–400.
85. For a fuller exposition of this case-study see Nigel Haigh and David Baldock, *Environmental Policy and 1992* (A report prepared for the British Department of the Environment on the consequences for environmental policy of the completion of the EC internal market, HMSO, 1989).

### Box 2: Small car emissions

Directive 83/351 set the standard of combined emissions of hydrocarbons (HC) and nitrogen oxides ($NO_x$) from small cars at 19g/test. This was to be reduced to 15g/test by 1990 under Directive 88/76.

> February 1988, European Commission proposal calls for a further reduction to 8g/test by 1992.

> EP first reading calls for standard of 5g/test (243 votes for, 63 against and 14 abstentions) in September 1988.

> Council split over standard: UK favours 12g/test; Germany 5g. On 24 November 1988, a standard of 8g/test formally adopted by Council by a qualified majority.

> At its second reading, the EP voted by an absolute majority (311 votes for, 5 against and 5 abstentions) to amend the Commission's proposal to a standard of 5g/test.

> Commission amends its proposal to 5g/test, as it had already declared it would do if the EP voted for that standard.

> Since Council required unanimity to restore the proposal standard to 8g, but only a qualified majority to adopt the amended proposal, a standard of 5g/test was adopted by Council on 9 June 1989 (Directive 89/458).

*Source*: Compiled by the author from information in Nigel Haigh and David Baldock, *Environmental Policy and 1992* (HMSO, 1989).

to change the directive substantially, with significant effects for consumers and car manufacturers across the Community.

One must not overstate the case; concrete examples of the EP's use of its new powers are rare. Yet this is not necessarily surprising if one remembers that MEPs are generally in favour of further integration and do not want to be seen as putting a brake on Community legislation. It should also be borne in mind that there has been an impact on the legislative programme in terms of speeding up legislation, and in the fact that a substantial number of parliamentary amendments are actually accepted by the Commission and Council.

The EP's second complete rejection of a proposal, in the sweeteners directive instance, also known as the 'Bangemann Footnote' (see Box 3), demonstrated the strength of a united Parliament. This case-study clearly shows the different stages a proposal goes through before reaching the statute books, but is also useful in showing the willingness of the EP to take on the Commission, and how cross-party links can work in ways which are unfamiliar to those used to the Westminster model of politics.

When the Council slipped a footnote into the proposals for a directive on sweeteners after it had been to the EP, the Parliament reacted strongly. The Socialist Chair of the Environment Committee, Ken Collins, and the EPP rapporteur, Caroline Jackson, took Commissioner Bangemann to task over the footnote, which ostensibly sought to protect traditional methods of beer-making in Germany, but was in fact an attempt at maintaining a trade barrier.

After a second parliamentary vote, the proposal was withdrawn by Bangemann.[86] There was some discussion as to whether the Commission actually had the right to withdraw a proposal at that stage. The Committee of Permanent Representatives (COREPER) continued to consider the proposals and in June 1994 the Council finally accepted Parliament's amendments. This case raised a further inter-institutional question on which Parliament pressed Commissioners-designate and President Santer in the confirmation hearings: what action would the Commission take if Parliament rejected proposed legislation or passed amendments by an absolute majority of Members? MEPs put considerable pressure on candidates to agree to cooperate by withdrawing proposals which Parliament had rejected by an absolute majority of members and by accepting amendments which it had adopted by

---

86. For a more detailed analysis see David Earnshaw and David Judge, 'The European Parliament and the Sweeteners Directive: From Footnote to Inter-Institutional Conflict', *Journal of Common Market Studies*, vol. 31, no. 1, March 1993, pp. 103–116.

**Box 3: Sweeteners directive**

December 1988, Council adopted a framework directive (89/107/EEC) on food additives. September 1990, Commission proposed a directive on sweeteners for use in foodstuffs within this framework.

Council consulted the European Parliament.

The EP referred the proposal to the Environment Committee. Thirty-four amendments to the proposal accepted. The plenary session in April 1991 largely accepted the report of rapporteur Caroline Jackson.

Commission agrees to 14 of the 39 amendments put forward by the EP, including a call for alcohol-free and low alcohol beers to be added to the list permitting sweeteners.

The EP had little impact on the Council's common position. However, a footnote relating to traditional methods in the production of low alcohol beers was added.

The common position was referred back to the Environment Committee. Jackson recommended the deletion of the footnote, but the Committee voted narrowly against her recommendation. The Economics Committee voted *for* deletion.

The common position was debated at the April plenary, but, at the request of the rapporteur, the vote was held over to the May plenary.

Box 3 cont.

Commissioner Bangemann essentially admitted to the EP that the footnote was a way of avoiding consulting Parliament afresh.

Belgium and the Netherlands let it be known that they were against the principle of exceptions for traditional foods, thereby giving the EP allies on the Council, so that a rejection of the common position could not be overruled.

The Environment Committee unanimously voted to propose a rejection of the common position in May. The plenary vote was two votes short of the absolute majority required for a rejection under the cooperation procedure. Jackson called for a second vote and the common position was finally rejected.

Bangemann immediately said that the Commission would withdraw its proposal.

COREPER continued to discuss the common position, even though the proposal on which it was based had been withdrawn. The Council finally accepted the proposal with Parliament's amendments in June 1994.

*Source*: compiled from the various reports and debates of the EP and David Earnshaw and David Judge, 'The European Parliament and the Sweeteners Directive: From Footnote to Inter-Institutional Conflict', *Journal of Common Market Studies*, vol. 31, no. 1, March 1993, pp. 103–16.

an absolute majority. The outcome, which gave MEPs limited grounds for satisfaction, was an agreement implying that it would need a decision of the full college of Commissioners in order not to follow Parliament's decision.

The TEU increases Parliament's powers in the legislative field further.[87] MEPs now have the right of co-decision with the Council in several policy areas under Article 189b. The new power relates only to fifteen Treaty items, but they cover broad areas including the majority of internal market legislation, public health, consumer protection, educational and cultural measures (see Appendix 1). Under this procedure, Parliament can reject certain items of legislation definitively. As with the cooperation procedure, the ultimate sanction — in this case the right to veto proposals — is not likely to be used frequently. What matters is the fact that the veto provision exists at all. In order to avoid the ultimate sanction of rejection, it is now necessary to achieve agreement earlier in the legislative process. A new Conciliation Committee, which brings together the Council and Parliament, has been created to facilitate the process.[88] This gives an opportunity for a compromise to be reached without Parliament having to make use of the ultimate sanction of rejection. It is possible that members of the institutions will attempt to achieve agreement at a much earlier stage in the proceedings, although this was not the case immediately following the 1994 elections.

The new procedure had been used prior to the 1994 elections. As a result of conciliation, agreement was reached in March on the Fourth Framework Programme for Research and Development. Parliament then narrowly failed to reject proposed legislation on the maximum brake horsepower of motorbikes, when only 252 of the requisite 260 members voted against the proposals. At the constitutive session of the incoming Parliament, MEPs were more successful, rejecting legislation on the liberalization of voice telephony under the telecom liberalization framework directive.[89] The motion to reject the proposal was passed by 375 votes to 45, with 12

---

87. See Richard Corbett, 'Increased Powers of the European Parliament,' *European Parliamentary Yearbook 1992/3*, pp. 20–3.
88. The committee excludes the Commission, a point which can be regarded as weakening the Commission's influence somewhat and was, naturally, a source of some contention.
89. Read Report on the text confirmed by the Council following the conciliation procedure on the proposal for a European Parliament and Council Directive on the application of open network provision to voice telephony [C4-0056/94] [A4-0001/94]. By voting in favour of the motion, MEPs rejected the Council's text.

abstentions. Apart from the symbolic importance of this occurrence, the reasons for the rejection of the proposed legislation are significant.

Although there were some differences between the Council and the EP about details of substance in the proposed legislation, they were relatively minor and could probably have been settled in the Conciliation Committee.[90] The real stumbling block was the Council's reluctance to tackle the problem of 'comitology' in European decision-making. At the most basic level, comitology can be seen to arise from 'the methods by which committees of civil servants from the member states review implementing decisions stemming from Directives'.[91] Although the Council had pledged to act on the issue, the EP accepted the advice of the rapporteur, Mel Read, who argued that no real progress had been made in this area. The fundamental problem is that in policy areas where Parliament has the right of co-decision in the primary legislation, it has no say in subsequent implementing legislation. The reasoning behind this situation is that the implementing decisions are purely technical; MEPs argue that this is not always so. In the voice telephony case, for instance, there is provision that blind people should be able to work in telephone exchanges. The introduction of visual display units would effectively exclude blind people from working in the exchanges, yet could get through as a technical point. Thus, Parliament feels it should have the right to a say on such implementing legislation.

In the six months after the elections, the issue of comitology was raised in several different conciliation procedures. While in several cases MEPs accepted the outcomes of the conciliation committees, generally arguing that the vast majority of their grievances had been met, the comitology issue continued to be a source of contention. Thus for example after many months the packaging directive was passed, with most of Parliament's amendments accepted and some concessions on comitology, but no permanent agreement on the issue.[92] Finally in December 1994 an interim agreement was reached whereby the committee which dealt with the primary legislation will be sent any proposed implementing acts and Council will not make a

---

90. The details of the various legislative procedures are laid out in Appendix 1.
91. This definition came from Mel Read, the rapporteur for the proposals, during an interview with the author on 22 July 1994.
92. The directive on packaging waste was accepted on 14 December 1994 [A4-113/94 – Jensen].

decision until the EP has expressed an opinion, subject to certain time limits.[93] This *modus vivendi* will be reviewed in 1996. Only with this question solved, at least in the short term, will it be possible to see how well the co-decision works in practice.

The Maastricht Treaty also extended the existing cooperation procedure to most areas of legislation where the Council uses qualified majority voting (QMV), with the marked exceptions of agricultural policy and external commerce. While it remains the case that MEPs cannot initiate legislation, they may now ask the Commission to propose legislation — a prerogative previously reserved for the Council. The right of initiative would obviously be a bonus for the EP, but even without it its powers in the legislative sphere have increased considerably over the years, and it should be remembered that very little legislation in national politics emerges from MPs directly. Moreover, MEPs can certainly influence the legislative process at an early stage; formal proposals must come from the Commission, but there is nothing to stop MEPs putting forward own-initiative reports to Parliament which can subsequently provide the basis for Commission proposals.

*4. Assent procedure*

The SEA increased the powers of the EP via the *assent procedure* which gives the EP the right to joint decision-making for accession and association agreements. Protocols with Israel were rejected on the basis of this procedure in 1988 and agreements with Turkey were delayed on human rights grounds in 1987. Parliament has enjoyed a limited benefit from this power so far, although it has exerted some influence on the Council.

The current rush of applications for membership of the Union greatly enhances the EP's scope for action. MEPs expressed their intention of using this power as a way of getting leverage to ensure a reduction in the democratic deficit which they claim exists in the Community (the solution for which, not inconsequentially, would mean an increase in parliamentary powers). Indeed, the German Foreign Minister, Klaus Kinkel, cited the EP's position as a reason for saying that the British and Spanish stance on qualified majority voting in Council was unacceptable. In the resolution on the results of the IGCs they declared that the EP

---

93. *Modus vivendi* between the European Parliament, the Council and the Commission concerning the implementing measures for acts adopted in accordance with the procedure laid down in Article 189b of the EC Treaty (PE 210.700/fin).

will not be able to agree to the accession of new member states unless further reforms are adopted in addition to the Maastricht Treaty, in particular concerning the democratic deficit and the consolidation of the principles and aims on which Political Union is based.[94]

However, when they actually voted on the accession of the Eftan applicant states in May 1994, MEPs gave overwhelming support to the agreements. This was despite the fact that the assent procedure (at least for accession agreements and the adoption of a common electoral system) requires an absolute majority of MEPs, usually 314 (formerly 260) to vote in favour.[95] As fewer than 500 MEPs are usually present at plenary sessions,[96] this is a fairly tall order, and one which could plausibly have blocked enlargement, whether by the positive will of parliamentarians anxious to press their claims for greater powers or by default, through insufficient attendance. In the event, MEPs felt that enlargement should not be blocked as a weapon to press for more powers.

A further problem arising from the majority provisions is that the relative sizes of the party groups means that EPP and PES groups must typically vote together to reach the requisite number of votes. This means it is particularly tricky for MEPs subsequently to distinguish themselves from their opponents when campaigning for re-election. In countries used to coalition government and consensus politics this may not be too much of a problem, but it is a difficult point to put across in Britain.

---

94. Resolution A3-0123/92 of the European Parliament.
95. On 4 May 1994 the EP voted on accession of the four applicant states (including Norway). The results for each of the countries were:

>   Norway – for: 374; against: 24; abstentions: 58.
>   Austria – for: 374; against: 24; abstentions: 61.
>   Finland – for: 377; against: 21; abstentions: 61.
>   Sweden – for: 380; against: 21; abstentions: 60.

See *Info Memo 1* (Brussels: EP Directorate General of the Press, 4 January 1995).
96. Although European electoral laws prohibit members of executives in any of the member states from sitting in the EP, the member states have each devised their own rules regarding incompatibilities. Where dual mandates are more common, such as in France and Italy, many well-known candidates gain seats in Strasbourg but rarely attend, attaching greater importance to their national political activities and helping ensure low rates of participation in plenary votes.

**Inter-institutional links**

Members of the other institutions traditionally regarded the EP with little interest. The Council had to wait until the Parliament had passed judgment on proposed legislation before it acted, but it rarely took any notice of the Parliament's opinions. At first legislation could undergo such significant changes in Council that it bore little relation to the Commission proposals on which the Parliamentary Committees were preparing their reports; and when the EP had reported the Council could simply adopt its own version of the proposal. This situation was altered by a decision by the European Court of Justice that Council must consult Parliament again if it alters legislation so that it bears little resemblance to the Commission proposal.

Parliamentary activities are followed closely by the Commission and, to a lesser extent, by members of COREPER. When the legislative process works well, 'behind-the-scenes' activity ensures that the various groups involved with the proposals keep themselves informed of just what members of the other institutions will accept and try to act accordingly. The introduction of the co-decision procedure has ensured that the Parliament and the Council must interact more than in the past. Indeed, the conciliation procedure introduced in the Maastricht Treaty excludes the Commission from the final decision: a source of annoyance to the Commission and a significant boost to Parliament's leverage in the decision-making process.

Similarly the cooperation procedure introduced by the Single European Act means increased interaction between the Parliament and the Commission at an early stage of the legislative process. Needless to say this does not always occur, but it seems that links are gradually improving. The new vote of approval of the Commission will further alter the relationship. It is even possible that eventually the selection of the Commission could be tied more closely to the EP elections, giving voters more of a sense that these elections actually do matter. The change is likely to cause a good deal of friction between Commission, Council and Parliament at least at first.

Even before such potential developments, however, the Parliament is attempting to alter the balance of relations with the other institutions. Both the Parliament and the Commission are aware of the potential which the right to vote on the incoming Commission gives the Parliament. The Commission hopes that the vote will endow it with the legitimacy which has frequently appeared to be lacking, as voters and politicians alike have focused on this bureaucratic body when seeking to criticize European enterprises. From the Parliament's perspective, although the provisions are still far from ideal, the hearings in January 1995 did enable MEPs to extract some concessions from the Commission President, not least in terms of the agreement to consider Parliament's demands that the Commission withdraw proposals rejected by an absolute majority of MEPs and accept amendments to proposed legislation adopted by an absolute majority of MEPs. Admittedly, the wording of this concession was not absolute, but M. Santer can expect harsh treatment from the Parliament if he does not act on these words.

Thus recent treaty changes have increased the role of the European Parliament, making it much harder to ignore. Further changes are to be expected in the short and medium term. As a result of the repeated disputes in co-decision legislation over the vexed question of 'comitology', Parliament finally secured an interim agreement which will be reconsidered in the Intergovernmental Conference and should give Parliament an enhanced role in the implementing legislation.

## Lobbyists and business

As the other institutions of the Union are beginning to appreciate its increased leverage, so too are many lobbyists.

As the case-studies above show, the parliament *can* affect the legislative output of the Community and hence have an impact on business interests and voters across the Union. As more legislation is undertaken at the European level, it becomes harder for individual countries to determine the outcome of legislation, particularly with the increased scope for qualified majority voting in Council. Quite apart from the contested issue of the 'democratic deficit', this means that lobbying national governments may no longer be enough. This problem is being highlighted by the fact that medium-sized, not just large, companies are increasingly lobbying in Brussels and Strasbourg. Although much lobbying still occurs at the national level, and that which occurs at the European level is still largely directed at the Commission, this is changing.

Reasons for lobbying the EP are varied. In some cases it comes about from a sense of what the EP might become, rather than because of its current power, but the number of amendments accepted suggests that this reason is gradually being replaced by a sense that MEPs can have an effect on legislation. In addition, the Parliament exerts influence informally on the Council and Commission and effective lobbyists can put their case to parliamentarians prior to formal meetings. Systematic lobbying of all MEPs is rarely undertaken. A good lobbyist will tend to target various categories of MEPs virtually regardless of nationality: those with constituency/regional interests overlapping the lobbyist's policy interests; rapporteurs in the committees dealing with their interests; key officials, such as party chairs and spokespeople; a few active parliamentarians, who may not have any official capacity on a particular committee but who are generally highly effective.

At a more local level, MEPs can lobby on behalf of their Euroconstituencies (in countries where there are no national lists) and voters can ask MEPs for assistance. As the Parliament makes decisions about the allocation of fairly large sums of money (such as the KONVER project for areas affected by the reduction in the defence industry), this can be important. However, it seems that few citizens are aware of who their MEP is or the activities he or she can undertake on their behalf, a situation which has been reflected in the European elections. Yet the impact of citizens can be important. In the motorbike speed case the rapporteur was able to glean important insights into the world of bikes from a group of bikers from several member states who arrived to lobby Parliament; conversely, the lobbyists were able to learn how best to make their views felt by contact with the rapporteur and committee. Thus citizens can be a useful asset to Parliament and in return can find a way of influencing decisions via MEPs.

**Summary**

The European Parliament has come a long way since the first direct elections in 1979. Its power and influence have increased and it is now taken much more seriously by the other European institutions. Yet these changes were not reflected by increased interest in the 1994 European elections. Turnout declined again, with the Netherlands and Portugal registering turnout lower than that of Britain for the first time. Nor did the issues raised seem to show any marked shift of focus towards European affairs. As in the past, it is the exception which proves the rule: the French electorate was offered an anti-Maastricht list and a list whose adherents were concerned with the war in Bosnia. Elsewhere, although issues concerning the European Union were sometimes raised, they scarcely formed the key focus of the campaigns.

Where does this leave the European Parliament? How might it evolve over the next five years, in particular in terms of the Intergovernmental Conference due in 1996?

# 5 BEYOND 1996

The European Parliament seeks to represent the citizens of Europe, yet the direct elections which were meant to confer on the European Community the democratic elements that previously seemed to be lacking have not caught the public's imagination. At the time of the first direct elections in 1979, the apparent lack of interest could plausibly be explained by the fact that the European Parliament had few powers and less influence. As we argued in the previous chapter, however, this reason is no longer sufficient, although it remains the case that, unlike most national elections, European Union elections do not offer the chance to change the government. The problem may be that, in the words of Joseph Weiler, the EU still lacks 'social legitimacy'.[97] This was most clearly demonstrated by the difficulties over ratification of the Maastricht Treaty encountered in several states.

If the lack of interest in European elections reflects attitudes towards the European Union as a political entity, not perceptions of the powers of the Parliament, a further problem emerges. MEPs are prone to assert that in order to overcome the problem which they see as the most important in the Union, namely the democratic deficit, they should be given more powers. The logic they use is that as one democratic institution (or set of institutions if we consider the fifteen national parliaments) loses power, another democratically elected institution should take over that power. This was certainly the idea behind the EP's accretion of budgetary and legislative powers. Yet if the Union lacks the support of its citizens, simply granting more powers to the EP will not necessarily help. The need to bring Europe closer to its people has never been more important and must be treated as more than a rhetorical statement.

---

97. Joseph H. H. Weiler, 'After Maastricht: Community Legitimacy in Post-1992 Europe', in William James Adams (ed.), *Singular Europe* (Michigan: University of Michigan Press, 1992).

One problem that the EU must address is that it seems to be remote from the citizens, partly as a result of decisions being taken in an ever larger political arena, where it becomes increasingly difficult for individuals to have any impact, even if there are direct elections. This is the price to be paid for the benefits of economic and/or political activity at a European, or even a global, level. Alongside this reduced influence, however, is a sense that the issues which are being tackled are ever more remote from the individual. In local politics, a voter can see how effective his/her representative is in clear ways, such as whether or not holes in the road are mended. At the European level this is much harder to see, especially when one considers that most European Union legislation must be put on the statute books via national legislatures.

Finally, since national politicians, both in legislatures and executives, jealously guard their powers (in some cases long after those powers have effectively gone), there is little incentive for them to inform voters that many of the activities previously undertaken at the national level are now tackled at the European level. Thus there are many reasons why the European Union has not yet achieved the legitimacy it craves, and why direct elections to the EP do not by themselves solve the problems.

In the face of all these hurdles, what might the European Parliament do to ensure its own legitimacy? In the first place, it could try to evoke voter interest in the elections by demonstrating how effectively it can act in the European decision-making process. Of course there are difficulties in this respect. It is difficult to get the media interested in transnational activities; thus little attention is paid either to the European elections or to the activities of the Parliament. As the Parliament's role grows, so many of the issues it tackles will gradually become more newsworthy, so helping it gain a degree of prominence, particularly if MEPs begin to tackle issues such as fraud which are of public concern. In order to speed up this process, the EP could push for a more effective information service. Much of the material already exists; what is needed is an improvement in the transmission network from offices to voters.

National politicians could certainly help as well by making clear that there are certain issues over which the national parliament no longer has the final say. Greater links between national and European parliaments could help this process, particularly if members of the respective institutions could be persuaded to see themselves as partners rather than rivals.

The media are also in a position to ameliorate the situation. While the absence of transnational media does impede the coverage of transnational events, it certainly does not preclude such reporting entirely; that depends on journalists and media magnates. Although the European Union may not be the most exciting topic, the impact that it exerts on the lives of hundreds of millions of people, often without their realization, means that it is surely an issue which journalists have a duty to take seriously.

The combination of these factors could lead to a greater sense of the importance of the European Union and perhaps encourage the gradual formation of a much stronger sense of European identity than currently exists. Naturally these changes cannot all be undertaken prior to 1996, but some movement in that direction could help to win popular support for the outcome of the IGC negotiations. Maastricht has left many legacies: it has raised (for the first time in some countries) the question of how far citizens want the process of European integration to go; it also led to a declaration by the German Constitutional Court to the effect that any further reforms of the EU treaties must be fully in accordance with the democratic principles of the German *Grundgesetz* (Basic Law).

The general message seems to be that politicians, both national and European, must proceed with caution. Given this proviso and the fact that some governments, notably the British, appear unwilling to countenance fundamental changes to the EU decision-making process, the EP may gain little from the IGC. Nevertheless certain changes are essential if an enlarged Union is to function at all, and all the institutions involved in the Groupe de Réflexion need to bear this in mind. It seems increasingly unlikely that the powers of the Union will be extended greatly in 1996, yet the EP may still be able to make gains.

Although much will depend on the overall blueprint for the Union adopted at the IGC, there are certain powers which the EP should seek, since they would serve both to interest the voters in European affairs and to make the Union more democratic.

(1) *The right to give a vote of confidence to individual Commissioners* – The chief problem with Article 158 is that, like the EP's power to censure the Commission, it is a blunt weapon. Parliament tried to maximize its influence with the introduction of individual hearings, but the fact that a vote had to be taken on the Commission as a whole quickly led to criticism of the Parliament. In the past it was felt that the Commission's collegiality should not be put into jeopardy by individual votes. However, there is nothing to stop Commissioners who have been individually confirmed in office

subsequently adhering to the principle of collective responsibility. Indeed, the fact that *all* of the Commissioners have been deemed competent should be taken by the Commission as a positive sign. An alternative, albeit less likely, approach would be for the Parliament to demand the right to nominate the Commission President itself. This choice would reflect the political balance of the elections, giving them a heightened importance.

(2) *The right of co-decision should be extended to all areas where the Council of Ministers takes decisions by qualified majority* – This would allow parliamentary scrutiny of all primary legislation, helping overcome the 'democratic deficit'. The problem of 'comitology' would persist, however, unless some further treaty revisions were made. To this end it would be desirable that some effort is made to create a hierarchy of European legislation, including constitutional, primary and implementing legislation.[98] In order to maximize the effects of this change, national parliaments should be given a larger say in European legislation, since this would serve the dual purpose of bringing the legislation a little closer to the people and also giving national politicians a reason to take an interest in European affairs. In particular, national parliaments should be part of decisions on constitutional change at an early stage, preferably working with the European Parliament, since this will help increase debate *before* decisions are taken.

The use of co-decision should be extended if an expanded Union is to be effective. In addition, Parliament ought to be able to recall implementing legislation arising from such primary legislation. This need not slow up the EU's decision-making processes very much, because Parliament could accept most of the proposals as they stand, but it would allow MEPs to prevent important decisions being made in committees which are accountable to no one.

A reduction of the number of legislative procedures would give voters at least some chance of understanding European decision-making and how they themselves can influence decisions.

---

98. This French concept was raised before the Maastricht Treaty negotiations and was the subject of an EP report (Report of the Committee of Institutional Affairs on the nature of Community acts, Rapporteur: Jean-Louis Bourlanges, A3-0085/91/Part B).

(3) *Parliament should be given similar powers in all aspects of the Community budget*, whether they relate to compulsory or non-compulsory spending. This would prevent unnecessary inter-institutional conflict and simplify proceedings.

Even if only some of these revisions are achieved in 1996, the Parliament's scope for action will be considerably increased. The effectiveness of any new powers will then depend on the MEPs; they will have to be extremely disciplined if they are to achieve their aims and act as the 'voice of the people'.

# APPENDIX I
## Legislative procedures in the European Union

**Co-decision Procedure – Article 189b**

Simple majority is required at first reading; a simple majority is needed to accept Council's common position at second reading, but an absolute majority of Parliament's component members is required to adopt a declaration of intent to reject the common position, or to amend or confirm the rejection of the common position. At third reading, a simple majority is needed to adopt a joint text, or an absolute majority of Parliament's component members to reject Council's text. There are two variants of the co-decision procedure:

(a) voting in Council is by unanimity;
(b) voting in Council is by qualified majority voting.

*Areas where co-decision applies*

| | |
|---|---|
| Art. 49 | freedom of movement of workers |
| Art. 54 | right of establishment |
| Art. 56(2) | harmonization of provisions as to foreign nationals |
| Art. 57(1) | mutual recognition of diplomas |
| Art. 57(2) | activities as self-employed persons (where unanimity is not specified) |
| Art. 66 | services |
| Art. 100a | internal market measures |
| Art. 100b | recognizing equivalence of a member state's provisions |
| Art. 126 | education |
| Art. 128 | culture* |
| Art. 129 | health |
| Art. 129a | consumer protection |
| Art. 129d | guidelines: trans-European networks |
| Art. 130i(1) | multiannual framework programme in research and development |
| Art. 130s(3) | environmental action programmes |

*Unanimity by Council required.

# APPENDIX I: LEGISLATIVE PROCEDURES IN THE EU § 99

## Cooperation Procedure – Article 189c

Simple majority is required to pass an amendment at first reading. At second reading, Parliament needs only a simple majority to accept Council's common position, but an absolute majority to reject or amend it.

*Areas where the cooperation procedure applies*

| | |
|---|---|
| Art. 6 | non-discrimination |
| Art. 75(1) | transport |
| Art. 125 | the Social Fund |
| Art. 127 | vocational training |
| Art. 129d | trans-European networks (except for guidelines) |
| Art. 130e | economic and social cohesion, implementing decisions |
| Art. 130o | research, implementation of programmes |
| Art. 130s(1&3) | the environment, action and implementation of programmes |
| Art. 130w | development cooperation |
| Art. 2(2) | social policy (protocol applying to all states except the UK) |

*In the area of economic and monetary union*

| | |
|---|---|
| Art. 103(5) | rules for multilateral surveillance procedure |
| Art. 104a | prohibition of privileged access to financial institutions |
| Art. 104b | prohibition of assumption of liability for commitments of public authorities |
| Art. 105a(2) | harmonization measures concerning the circulation of coins |

## Assent Procedure

A simple majority is sufficient except for Art. 138 (electoral procedure) and Art. O (formerly Art. 237 – accession agreements) where an absolute majority of component Members of Parliament is necessary.

*Areas where the assent procedure applies*

| | |
|---|---|
| Art. 8a | citizenship |
| Art. 130d | Structural Funds |
| Art. 130d(2) | Cohesion Funds |
| Art. 138 | election procedure |
| Art. 228 | international agreements, including association agreements (former Art. 238) and cooperation agreements, or agreements with significant budgetary implications or implying the modification of decisions taken under the co-decision procedure (for remaining areas, with the exception of Art. 113(3), the consultation procedure applies) |

*In the area of economic and monetary union*
Art. 105(6)     specific tasks of the European Central Bank relating to supervision
Art. 106(5)     amendment of the protocol of the European System of Central Banks

**Consultation Procedure**

Simple majority is required in Parliament. There are two variants:

(a) voting in Council is by unanimity;
(b) voting in Council is by qualified majority voting.

*Areas where consultation applies*
Art. 8b            citizenship
Art. 8e            citizenship (ratification by member states)
Art. 75(3)         transport
Art. 100           harmonization of legislation
Art. 100c          entry and residence of third country nations
Art. 130(3)        industry
Art. 130b          cohesion
Art. 130i(4)       research – specific programmes
Art. 130o(part)    research
Art. 130s(2)       environment
Art. J(7)          information and consultation on a Common Foreign and Security Policy
Art. K(6)          information and consultation on Justice and Home Affairs
Art. 2(3)          social policy (agreement applying to all states except the UK)

*In the area of economic and monetary union*
Art. 104c(14)      revision of the protocol on excessive deficits
Art. 106(6)        adoption of the Statute of the European System of Central Banks
Art. 109(1)        European Currency Unit exchange rates
Art. 109a(4)       appointment of the President of the European Central Bank
Art. 109f(1)       appointment of the President of the European Monetary Institute
Art. 109f(6)       rules for consultation of the European Monetary Institute by the Council
Art. 109f(7)       other tasks of the European Monetary Institute
Art. 109j(2)       beginning of the third stage of EMU
Art. 109k(1)       derogations in EMU
Art. 109k(2)       abrogation of derogations
Art. 109l(1)       adoption of certain provisions of the Statute of the European System of Central Banks

*Source*: Adapted from *Report of the Committee of Institutional Affairs on the results of the intergovernmental conferences* (PE 155.444/fin./Party 11).

# APPENDIX 2
## Summary of key points of Parliament's rules of procedure which have been revised to take into account changes under the Maastricht Treaty

(1) *Introduction of the co-decision procedure into the rules* (Ams. 25–50): these amendments:

- adapt the existing procedures for 1st and 2nd reading;
- introduce the new stage of 'intention to reject common positions';
- provide for the establishment of Parliament's conciliation delegation (to include the chairman and rapporteur of the committee responsible, 3 permanent members appointed on an annual basis among the vice-presidents who will attend all conciliation meetings, and other members to make up the numbers in proportion to the size of political groups);
- to provide for a 3rd reading (worded in such a way as to discourage Council from adopting texts unilaterally in 3rd reading).

(2) *Adjustment of the assent procedure*: this is adapted to provide for the greater scope of the procedure and the various majorities now required. Assent on enlargements would be given after negotiations are concluded, but before Council signs. For legislative assents, if Parliament approves 'recommendations' with the same majority as required for the final assent, it may request conciliation with Council.

(3) *General improvements to the legislative procedures* (1st and 2nd readings) (Ams. 26–28): these procedures are tightened up, notably by requiring the Commission to give its position on amendments at committee stage already. Committees should verify the legal base of proposals before the substance, but questions on subsidiarity, fundamental rights and financial cover would be dealt with at the same time as the substance of proposals. The Legal Affairs Committee must be consulted on challenges to the legal base.

(4) *Appointment of the President and members of the Commission* (Ams. 16–17): the proposed candidate for the President will be requested to make a statement to plenary followed by a debate in which Council will be invited to take part. Approval shall be by a simple majority. Regarding the Commission as a whole, the various candidates will be requested to appear before the appropriate committee according to the prospective field of responsibility. The President-designate shall present the

programme of the Commission to Parliament for a debate. Approval or non-approval of the Commission shall be by a simple majority.

(5) *Other appointments* (Ams. 19 & 63): candidates for the Presidency of the Central Bank, members of its Board, the Presidency of the Monetary Institute and members of the Court of Auditors will be invited to appear before the responsible parliamentary committee, which shall make a recommendation to plenary. If the candidate is rejected the President shall ask the Council to withdraw a proposal and make a new one.

(6) *Annual Legislative Programme* (Am. 23): this will be negotiated earlier than at present (before the end of the previous year) after a debate and vote in Parliament on the Commission's Annual Work Programme. The Commission and Parliament agree on an Annual Legislative Programme including pre-legislative documents and agreements with third countries. Council will be invited to participate in this procedure. Negotiations are to be concluded through the Presidents of the institutions.

(7) *Common Foreign and Security Policy* (Ams. 90, 91, 92 & 113): the term EPC (European Political Cooperation) is abolished throughout the rules. Commission and Council should inform Parliament 'fully and in good time'. Parliament may adopt recommendations. Shorter deadlines than for other fields are provided e.g. for questions, and a simplified procedure is provided for the adoption of recommendations.

(8) *Justice and Home Affairs* (Am. 96): similar provisions as for CFSP.

(9) *Ombudsman* (Ams. 99, 100 & 101): appointment by Parliament on a proposal of committee responsible. Nominations to committee by 23 or more members. Powers of the ombudsman to be included in an annex to the rules proposed by the ombudsman and approved by Parliament. Confidentiality is provided.

(10) *Temporary Committees of Inquiry* (Ams. 845): Committees of up to 15 members and up to 9 months. Rules follow Treaty language and refer to necessary inter-institutional agreement. Provision made for confidentiality.

(11) *Discharge* (Am. 109 & 64): new provision to bring action before Court for failure to comply with Parliament's comments accompanying the discharge.

*Source*: Reproduced from a document by Richard Corbett (PE/GS 234.93, 30 September 1993).

# APPENDIX 3
## Committees in the European Parliament as at 18 January 1995

| | |
|---|---|
| C1 | Foreign Affairs, Security and Defence Policy (61 members) |
| C2 | Agriculture and Rural Development (49 members) |
| C3 | Budgets (38 members) |
| C4 | Economic and Monetary Affairs and Industrial Policy (57 members) |
| C5 | Research, Technological Development and Energy (31 members) |
| C6 | External Economic Relations (28 members) |
| C7 | Legal Affairs and Citizens' Rights (26 members) |
| C8 | Social Affairs and Employment (48 members) |
| C9 | Regional Policy (42 members) |
| C10 | Transport and Tourism (39 members) |
| C11 | Environment, Public Health and Consumer Protection (50 members) |
| C12 | Culture, Youth, Education and the Media (39 members) |
| C13 | Development and Cooperation (37 members) |
| C14 | Civil Liberties and Internal Affairs (35 members) |
| C15 | Budgetary Control (27 members) |
| C16 | Institutional Affairs (45 members) |
| C17 | Fisheries (25 members) |
| C18 | Rules of Procedure, the Verification of Credentials and Immunities (26 members) |
| C19 | Women's Rights (41 members) |
| C20 | Petitions (29 members) |
| | Temporary Committee on Employment (41 members) |

*Source*: European Parliament Minutes of the sitting of Wednesday 18 January 1995 (PE 186.410).

# APPENDIX 4
## Tables of votes and seats for the Member States in European and national elections*

### Belgium

| Party | Group in EP July 1994 | 1979 votes % | 1979 seats | 1984 votes % | 1984 seats | 1989 votes % | 1989 seats | 1994 votes % | 1994 seats | National (Nov. 1991) votes % | National (Nov. 1991) seats |
|---|---|---|---|---|---|---|---|---|---|---|---|
| Flemish Socialist Party (SP) | PES | 12.8 | 3 | 17.1 | 4 | 12.4 | 3 | 10.8 | 3 | 12.0 | 28 |
| Walloon Parti Socialiste (PS) | PES | 10.6 | 4 | 13.3 | 5 | 14.5 | 5 | 11.3 | 3 | 13.5 | 35 |
| Christian People's Party (CVP) | EPP | 29.5 | 7 | 19.8 | 4 | 21.1 | 5 | 17.0 | 4 | 16.8 | 39 |
| Christian Social Party (PSC) | EPP | 8.2 | 3 | 7.6 | 2 | 8.1 | 2 | 6.9 | 2 | 7.7 | 18 |
| Flemish Liberals and Democrats (VLD) | ELDR | 9.4 | 2 | 8.6 | 2 | 10.6 | 2 | 11.4 | 3 | 12.0 | 26 |
| Liberal Reform Party (PRL) | ELDR | 6.9 | 2 | 9.4 | 3 | 7.2 | 2 | 9.0 | 3 | 8.1 | 20 |
| Volksunie (VU) | ERA | 6.0 | 1 | 8.5 | 2 | 5.4 | 1 | 4.4 | 1 | 5.9 | 10 |
| Agalev | Greens | 1.4 | — | 4.3 | 1 | 7.6 | 1 | 6.7 | 1 | 4.9 | 7 |
| Ecolo | Greens | 2.0 | — | 3.9 | 1 | 6.3 | 2 | 4.8 | 1 | 5.1 | 10 |
| Vlaams Blok | Non-attached | 0.7 | — | 1.3 | — | 4.1 | — | 7.8 | 2 | 6.6 | 12 |
| Christian Social Party (German) | EPP | — | — | — | — | — | — | 0.2 | 1 | — | — |
| National Front | Non-attached | — | — | — | — | — | — | 2.9 | — | — | — |
| Others | | 12.5 | 2 | 6.1 | — | 3.0 | — | 6.9 | — | 6.7 | 7 |
| Turnout (%) | | 91.4 | | 92.2 | | 90.7 | | 90.7 | | 92.0 | |

25 seats in the European Parliament (24 until 1994) (divided into Flanders – 14 seats; Wallonia – 10; German speaking – 1)
212 seats in the Chamber of Representatives

*For all tables in this Appendix, figures have been rounded; sources are: *Info Memo 'Special Elections' Nos. 1-2* (Brussels, EP, 1994); *Results and Elected Members provisional edition*, 15 June 1994 (Brussels, EP, 1994); *'Special Elections' XVIII Session Constitutive le Nouveau PE au 19 Juillet* (Brussels, EP. 1994).

## Denmark

| Party | Group in EP 1994 | 1979 votes % | 1979 seats | 1984 votes % | 1984 seats | 1989 votes % | 1989 seats | 1994 votes % | 1994 seats | National (Sept. 1994) votes % | National (Sept. 1994) seats |
|---|---|---|---|---|---|---|---|---|---|---|---|
| Social Democrats | PES | 21.9 | 3 | 19.5 | 3 | 23.3 | 4 | 15.8 | 3 | 34.6 | 62 |
| People's Movement Against the EU | EN | 20.9 | 4 | 20.8 | 4 | 18.9 | 4 | 10.3 | 2 | — | — |
| Conservative People's Party | EPP | 14.0 | 2 | 20.8 | 4 | 13.3 | 2 | 17.7 | 3 | 15.0 | 27 |
| Venstre | ELDR | 14.5 | 3 | 12.5 | 2 | 16.6 | 3 | 19.0 | 4 | 23.2 | 42 |
| Socialist People's Party | Greens | 4.7 | 1 | 9.2 | 2 | 9.1 | 1 | 8.6 | 1 | 7.3 | 13 |
| Centre Democrats | | 6.2 | 1 | 6.6 | 1 | 7.9 | 2 | 0.9 | — | 2.8 | 5 |
| Progress Party | | 5.8 | 1 | 3.5 | — | 5.3 | — | 2.9 | — | 6.4 | 11 |
| Det Radikale Venstre | ELDR | — | — | — | — | 2.8 | — | 8.5 | 1 | 4.6 | 8 |
| June Movement | EN | — | — | — | — | — | — | 15.2 | 2 | — | — |
| Unity List (Red/Green Alliance) | | — | — | — | — | — | — | — | — | 3.2 | 6 |
| Others | | 12.0 | — | 7.1 | 1 | 2.8 | — | 1.1 | — | 2.9 | 1 |
| Turnout (%) | | 47.8 | | 52.4 | | 46.2 | | 52.5 | | | |

16 seats in the European Parliament
179 seats in the Folketing (including four from Greenland and the Faroe Isles not listed here)

## Germany

| Party | Group in EP 1994 | 1979 votes % | 1979 seats | 1984 votes % | 1984 seats | 1989 votes % | 1989 seats | 1994 votes % | 1994 seats | National (Oct. 1994) votes % | National (Oct. 1994) seats |
|---|---|---|---|---|---|---|---|---|---|---|---|
| Social Democratic Party (SPD) | PES | 40.8 | 35 | 37.4 | 33 | 37.3 | 31 | 32.2 | 40 | 36.4 | 252 |
| Christian Democratic Union (CDU) | EPP | 39.1 | 34 | 37.5 | 34 | 29.5 | 25 | 32.0 | 39 | 34.2 | 244 |
| Christian Social Union (CSU) | EPP | 10.1 | 8 | 8.5 | 7 | 8.2 | 7 | 6.8 | 8 | 7.3 | 50 |
| Free Democrats (FDP) | | 6.0 | 4 | 4.8 | — | 5.6 | 4 | 4.1 | — | 6.9 | 47 |
| Party of Democratic Socialism (PDS) | | — | — | — | — | — | — | 4.7 | — | 4.4 | 30 |
| Greens | Greens | 3.2 | — | 8.2 | 7 | 8.4 | 8 | 10.1 | 12 | 7.3 | 49 |
| Republicans | | — | — | — | — | 7.1 | — | 3.9 | — | 1.9 | 0 |
| Others | | 0.8 | — | 3.6 | — | 3.9 | — | 6.2 | — | 1.1 | 0 |
| Turnout (%) | | 65.7 | | 56.8 | | 62.3 | | 60.1 | | 79.1 | |

99 seats in European Parliament (81 until 1994)

NB the number of seats in the Bundestag is subject to minor variations dependent on electoral regulations.

Sources for 1994 German election results: David Marsh, *Germany After the Elections: What Now for Europe?*, RIIA Briefing Paper No. 12, October 1994; German Embassy, London.

## Greece

| Party | Group in EP 1994 | 1981 votes % | 1981 seats | 1984 votes % | 1984 seats | 1989 votes % | 1989 seats | 1994 votes % | 1994 seats | National (Oct. 1993) votes % | National (Oct. 1993) seats |
|---|---|---|---|---|---|---|---|---|---|---|---|
| Pasok | PES | 40.1 | 10 | 41.6 | 10 | 36.0 | 9 | 37.6 | 10 | 46.9 | 170 |
| New Democracy | EPP | 31.3 | 8 | 38.1 | 9 | 40.4 | 10 | 32.7 | 9 | 39.3 | 111 |
| Left Coalition and Progress* | | — | — | — | — | 14.3 | 4 | — | — | — | — |
| Communist Party of Greece (KKE) | United Left | 12.8 | 3 | 11.6 | 3 | — | — | 6.3 | 2 | 4.5 | 9 |
| Left Alliance (SYN) | United Left | 5.3 | 1 | 3.4 | 1 | — | — | 6.3 | 2 | — | — |
| Progress | | 1.2 | 1 | — | — | — | — | — | — | — | — |
| Political Spring | | — | — | — | — | — | — | 8.7 | 2 | 4.9 | 10 |
| Centre Right Alliance (DIANA) | EDA | — | — | — | — | 1.4 | 1 | 2.8 | — | — | — |
| Epen | | — | — | 2.3 | 1 | 1.2 | — | — | — | — | — |
| Kodiso | | 4.2 | 1 | — | — | — | — | — | — | — | — |
| Others | | 4.7 | — | 3 | — | 6.7 | — | 5.6 | — | 4.4 | — |
| Turnout (%) | | 78.6 | | 77.2 | | 79.9 | | 71.2 | | 81.5 | |

25 seats in European Parliament (24 until 1994)
300 seats in the Vouli

* Includes a KKE MEP

## Spain

| Party | Group in EP 1994 | 1987 votes % | 1987 seats | 1989 votes % | 1989 seats | 1994 votes % | 1994 seats | National (June 1993) votes % | National (June 1993) seats |
|---|---|---|---|---|---|---|---|---|---|
| Socialist Workers' Party (PSOE) | PES | 39.1 | 28 | 40.2 | 27 | 30.7 | 22 | 38.6 | 159 |
| Popular Party (PP) | EPP | 24.7 | 17 | 21.7 | 15 | 40.2 | 28 | 34.8 | 141 |
| United Left (IU) | United Left | 5.2 | 3 | 6.2 | 4 | 13.5 | 9 | 9.5 | 18 |
| Catalan Party | EPP (1) | — | — | — | — | — | — | — | — |
| Democrat and Social Centre | ELDR (2) | 4.4 | 3 | 4.3 | 2 | 4.7 | 3 | 5.0 | 17 |
| Nationalist Coalition | | 10.3 | 7 | 7.2 | 5 | 1.0 | — | — | — |
| (regional parties) | EPP/ERA | — | — | 1.9 | 1 | 2.8 | 2 | — | — |
| European People's Coalition | | 1.7 | 1 | 1.5 | — | 1.3 | — | — | — |
| Andalucian Party | | 1.0 | — | 1.9 | — | 0.8 | — | — | — |
| Regional Left Party | | 1.3 | — | 1.9 | — | — | — | — | — |
| Basque Party (Herri Batasuna) | | 1.9 | 1 | 1.7 | 1 | 1.0 | — | 0.8 | 2 |
| Supporters of Ruiz Mateos | | — | — | 3.9 | 2 | — | — | — | — |
| Galicia National Party | | — | — | — | — | 0.8 | — | — | — |
| Greens | | — | — | — | — | 0.7 | — | — | — |
| Others | | 10.4 | — | 7.8 | — | 2.4 | — | 11.4 | 13 |
| Turnout (%) | | 68.9 | | 54.6 | | 59.6 | | 77.3 | |

64 seats in European Parliament (60 until 1994)
350 seats in the Congress of Deputies

## France

| Party | Group in EP 1994 | 1979 votes % | 1979 seats | 1984 votes % | 1984 seats | 1989 votes % | 1989 seats | 1994 votes % | 1994 seats | National (March 1993) votes % | National (March 1993) seats |
|---|---|---|---|---|---|---|---|---|---|---|---|
| Socialists (PS) | PES | 23.5 | 22 | 20.8 | 20 | 23.6 | 22 | 14.5 | 15 | 19.2 | 49 |
| UDF/RPR (joint list) | (EPP, 13) (ELDR, 1) (EDA, 14) | — | — | 43.0 | 41 | — | — | 25.6 | 28 | — | — |
| RPR/Giscardian list | | — | — | — | — | 28.9 | 26 | — | — | — | — |
| Centre/Veil list | | — | — | — | — | 8.4 | 7 | — | — | — | — |
| RPR | | 16.3 | 15 | — | — | — | — | — | — | 20.4 | 246 |
| UDF | | 27.6 | 25 | — | — | — | — | — | — | 19.1 | 213 |
| L'Autre Europe (De Villiers list) | EN | — | — | — | — | — | — | 12.3 | 13 | — | — |
| Energie Radicale (Tapie) | ERA | — | — | — | — | — | — | 12.0 | 13 | — | — |
| Front National | Non-attached | 1.3 | — | 11.0 | 10 | 11.7 | 10 | 10.5 | 11 | 12.5 | — |
| Communist Party (PCF) | United Left | 20.5 | 19 | 11.2 | 10 | 7.7 | 7 | 6.9 | 7 | 9.1 | 23 |
| Greens | | 4.4 | — | 3.4 | — | 10.6 | 9 | 4.9 | — | 4.0 | — |
| Others | | 6.3 | — | 10.7 | — | 9.1 | — | 13.3 | — | 15.7 | 46 |
| Turnout (%) | | 60.7 | | 56.7 | | 48.7 | | 52.7 | | 69.0 | |

87 seats in European Parliament (81 until 1994)
577 seats in the Assemblée Nationale

# Ireland

| Party | Group in EP 1994 | 1979 votes % | 1979 seats | 1984 votes % | 1984 seats | 1989 votes % | 1989 seats | 1994 votes % | 1994 seats | National (Nov. 1992) votes % | National (Nov. 1992) seats |
|---|---|---|---|---|---|---|---|---|---|---|---|
| Fianna Fáil | EDA | 34.7 | 5 | 39.2 | 8 | 31.5 | 6 | 35.0 | 7 | 39.1 | 68 |
| Fine Gael | EPP | 33.0 | 4 | 32.2 | 6 | 21.6 | 4 | 24.3 | 4 | 24.5 | 45 |
| Labour | PES | 14.5 | 4 | 8.4 | — | 9.5 | 1 | 11.0 | 1 | 19.3 | 33 |
| Greens | Greens | — | — | 0.5 | — | 3.8 | — | 7.9 | 2 | 1.4 | 1 |
| Independent | ELDR | 14.3 | 2 | 13.1 | 1 | 6.8 | 2 | 6.9 | 1 | — | — |
| Progressive Democrats | | — | — | — | — | 12.0 | 1 | 6.5 | — | 4.7 | 10 |
| Democratic Left | | — | — | — | — | 7.5 | — | 3.5 | — | 2.8 | 4 |
| Others | | 3.5 | — | 6.4 | — | 7.3 | — | 4.9 | — | 8.2 | 5 |
| Turnout (%) | | 63.6 | | 47.6 | | 68.3 | | 44.0 | | 68.5 | |

15 seats in European Parliament
166 seats in the Dáil

## Italy

| Party | Group in EP 1994 | 1979 votes % | 1979 seats | 1984 votes % | 1984 seats | 1989 votes % | 1989 seats | 1994 votes % | 1994 seats | National (March 1994) votes % | National (March 1994) seats |
|---|---|---|---|---|---|---|---|---|---|---|---|
| Forza Italia | FE | — | — | — | — | — | — | 30.6 | 27 | } 42.9 | 366 |
| Northern League | ELDR | — | — | — | — | 1.8 | 2 | 6.6 | 6 | | |
| National Alliance (ex-MSI) | Non-attached | 5.4 | 4 | 6.5 | 5 | 5.5 | 4 | 12.5 | 11 | | |
| Party of the Democratic Left (PDS) | PES | 29.6 | 24 | 33.3 | 27 | 27.6 | 22 | 19.1 | 16* | } 32.2 | 213 |
| Refounded Communists | United Left | — | — | — | — | — | — | 6.1 | 5 | | |
| Italian Popular Party (ex-Christian Democrats) | EPP | 36.4 | 29 | 33.0 | 26 | 32.9 | 26 | 10.0 | 8 | } 15.7 | 46 |
| Segni List (ex-Christian Democrats) | EPP | — | — | — | — | — | — | 3.3 | 3 | | |
| Radicals, Liberals and Republicans | ELDR (1) ERA (2) | 9.9 | 8 | 9.5 | 8 | 4.4 | 4 | 3.0 | 3 | | |
| Greens | Greens | — | — | — | — | 6.2 | 5 | 3.2 | 3 | | |
| Socialist Party (PSI-AD) | PES | 11.0 | 9 | 11.2 | 9 | 14.8 | 12 | 1.8 | 2 | | |
| Social Democratic Party (PSDI) | Non-attached | 4.3 | 4 | 3.5 | 3 | 2.7 | 2 | 0.7 | 1 | | |
| Others (mainly regional) | EPP (1) Greens (1) | 3.4 | 3 | 3.0 | 3 | 4.1 | 4 | 3.1 | 2 | 9.2 | 5 |
| Turnout (%) | | 84.9 | | 83.4 | | 81.0 | | 74.8 | | 86.1 | |

87 seats in European Parliament (81 until 1994)
630 seats in the Chamber of Deputies
* with anti-mafia network and others

# Luxembourg

| Party | Group in EP 1994 | 1979 votes % | 1979 seats | 1984 votes % | 1984 seats | 1989 votes % | 1989 seats | 1994 votes % | 1994 seats | National (June 1994) votes % | National (June 1994) seats |
|---|---|---|---|---|---|---|---|---|---|---|---|
| Christian Social People's Party (CSV) | EPP | 36.1 | 3 | 34.9 | 3 | 34.9 | 3 | 31.4 | 2 | 29.5 | 21 |
| Socialist Workers' Party (LSAP) | PES | 21.7 | 1 | 29.9 | 2 | 25.4 | 2 | 24.8 | 2 | 30.4 | 17 |
| Democratic Party (DP) | ELDR | 28.1 | 2 | 22.1 | 1 | 20.0 | 1 | 18.9 | 1 | 14.5 | 12 |
| Green list | Greens | — | — | 6.1 | — | 10.4 | — | 10.9 | 1 | 10.1 | 5 |
| Communists (KPL) |  | 5.0 | — | 4.1 | — | 4.7 | — | — | — | 2.4 | — |
| ADR (formerly 5/6 Action Committee) |  | — | — | — | — | — | — | — | — | 7.7 | 5 |
| Others |  | 9.1 | — | 2.9 | — | 4.6 | — | 14.0 | — | 5.4 | — |
| Turnout (%) |  | 88.9 |  | 88.8 |  | 87.4 |  | 88.5 |  | 88.3 |  |

6 seats in European Parliament
60 seats in the Chamber of Deputies

*Sources for 1994 election results: D Hearl, 'Notes on the Elections to the European Parliament', *Electoral Studies 1994*, vol. 13, no. 4; Luxembourg Embassy, London.

*Note:* There were two different electoral registers used for the European and national elections, though differences were very minor.

## Netherlands

| Party | Group in EP 1994 | 1979 votes % | 1979 seats | 1984 votes % | 1984 seats | 1989 votes % | 1989 seats | 1994 votes % | 1994 seats | National (May 1994) votes % | National (May 1994) seats |
|---|---|---|---|---|---|---|---|---|---|---|---|
| Christian Democrats (CDA) | EPP | 35.6 | 10 | 30.0 | 8 | 34.6 | 10 | 30.8 | 10 | 22.2 | 34 |
| Labour Party (PvdA) | PES | 30.4 | 9 | 33.7 | 9 | 30.7 | 8 | 22.9 | 8 | 24.0 | 37 |
| Freedom and Democracy Party (VVD) | ELDR | 16.2 | 4 | 18.9 | 5 | 13.6 | 3 | 17.9 | 6 | 19.9 | 31 |
| Democrats 66 (D'66) | ELDR | 9.0 | 2 | 2.3 | — | 5.9 | 1 | 11.7 | 4 | 15.5 | 24 |
| Green (Rainbow list in 1984 and 1989) | Greens | — | — | 5.6 | 2 | 7.0 | 2 | 6.1 | 1 | 3.5 | 5 |
| Coalition of Orthodox Protestants | EN | — | — | 5.2 | 1 | 5.9 | 1 | 7.8 | 2 | 4.8* | 7 |
| General Association for the Elderly | | | | | | | | — | — | 3.6 | 6 |
| Others | | 8.8 | — | 4.3 | — | 2.3 | — | 2.8 | — | 6.5 | 6 |
| Turnout (%) | | 57.8 | | 50.6 | | 47.2 | | 35.6 | | 78.3 | |

31 seats in European Parliament (25 until 1994)
150 seats in the Tweede Kamer

Source for 1994 results – Royal Netherlands Embassy, London

* This figure is the sum of votes for the Calvinist Party (SGP), the Reformed Political League (GPV) and the Evangelical Political Federation (RPF).

## Portugal

| Party | Group in EP 1994 | 1987 votes % | 1987 seats | 1989 votes % | 1989 seats | 1994 votes % | 1994 seats | National (Oct. 1991) votes % | National (Oct. 1991) seats |
|---|---|---|---|---|---|---|---|---|---|
| Social Democratic Party (PSD) | ELDR (8) | 38.4 | 10 | 32.7 | 9 | 34.4 | 9 | 50.6 | 135 |
| Socialist Party (PS) | EPP (1) PES | 23.1 | 6 | 28.5 | 8 | 34.8 | 10 | 29.1 | 72 |
| United Democratic Alliance (CDU) | United Left | 11.8 | 3 | 14.4 | 4 | 11.2 | 3 | 8.1 | 17 |
| Social Democratic Centre (CDS) | EDA | 15.8 | 4 | 14.1 | 3 | 12.5 | 3 | 4.4 | 5 |
| Others (incl. invalid papers) | | 10.9 | 1 | 10.3 | — | 7.1 | — | 7.1 | 1 |
| Turnout (%) | | 72.6 | | 51.2 | | 35.6 | | 68.2 | |

25 seats in the European Parliament (24 until 1994)
230 seats in the Assembly of the Republic

## United Kingdom

| Party | Group in EP 1994 | 1979 votes % | 1979 seats | 1984 votes % | 1984 seats | 1989 votes % | 1989 seats | 1994 votes % | 1994 seats | National (April 1992) votes % | National (April 1992) seats |
|---|---|---|---|---|---|---|---|---|---|---|---|
| Labour | PES | 31.6 | 17 | 36.5 | 32 | 40.1 | 45 | 42.7 | 62 | 34.4 | 271 |
| Conservatives | EPP | 48.4 | 60 | 40.8 | 45 | 34.1 | 32 | 26.8 | 18 | 41.9 | 336 |
| Scottish National Party (SNP) | ERA | 1.9 | 1 | 1.7 | 1 | 2.7 | 1 | 3.1 | 2 | 1.9 | 3 |
| Liberal Democrats | ELDR | 12.6 | — | 19.5 | — | 6.4 | — | 16.1 | 2 | 17.8 | 20 |
| Greens | | — | — | 0.6 | — | 15.0 | — | 3.1 | — | — | — |
| Plaid Cymru | | 0.6 | — | 0.7 | — | 0.8 | — | 1.0 | — | 0.5 | 1 |
| Democratic Ulster Unionists (DUP) | Non-attached | 1.3 | 1 | 1.6 | 1 | 1.0 | 1 | 1.0 | 1 | 2.2* | 3 |
| Social Democratic and Labour Party (SDLP) | PES | 1.1 | 1 | 1.1 | 1 | 0.9 | 1 | 1.0 | 1 | | 4 |
| Official Ulster Unionist Party (OUP) | EPP | 0.9 | 1 | 1.1 | 1 | 0.8 | 1 | 0.8 | 1 | | 9 |
| Others | | 1.6 | — | 0.9 | — | 1.5 | — | 4.4 | — | 1.3 | 4 |
| Turnout (%) | | 32.3 | | 32.6 | | 36.2 | | 36.4† | | 77.7 | |

87 seats in the European Parliament (81 until 1994) of which 3 are elected by STV in Northern Ireland
651 seats in the House of Commons

*Northern Ireland accounts for 2.2% of the votes cast and 17 seats in the House of Commons.
†Turnout was 48.7% in Northern Ireland and 36.1% in the rest of UK.

## Austria: national elections, October 1994

|  | Votes (%) | Seats | Seats in EP |
|---|---|---|---|
| Social Democratic Party (PES) | 35 | 66 | 8 |
| People's Party (EPP) | 28 | 52 | 6 |
| Freedom Party (NA) | 23 | 42 | 5 |
| Greens (Greens) | 7 | 13 | 1 |
| Liberal Forum (ELDR) | 5 | 10 | 1 |
| Total |  | 183 | 21 |

Sources: *Info Memo 1* (Brussels: European Parliament – Directorate of the Press, 4 January 1995) and *The Guardian* (10 October 1994).

## Finland: national elections, 1991

|  | Votes (%) | Seats | Seats in EP |
|---|---|---|---|
| Centre Party (ELDR) | 27.5 | 55 | 5 |
| Social Democrats (PES) | 24.0 | 48 | 4 |
| National Coalition Party (EPP) | 20.5 | 41 | 4 |
| Left-Wing Alliance (United Left) | 9.5 | 19 | 1 |
| Swedish People's Party (ELDR) | 6.0 | 12 | 1 |
| Greens (Greens) | 5.0 | 10 | 1 |
| Other | 7.5 | 15 | — |
| Total |  | 200 | 16 |

Source: *Info Memo 1* (Brussels: EP – Directorate of the Press, 4 January 1995).

## Sweden: national elections, September 1994

|  | Votes (%) | Seats | Seats in EP |
|---|---|---|---|
| Social Democrats (PES) | 46 | 161 | 11 |
| Moderate Party (EPP) | 23 | 80 | 5 |
| Centre Party (ELDR) | 8 | 27 | 2 |
| Liberal People's Party (ELDR) | 8 | 26 | 1 |
| Left Party (United Left) | 6 | 22 | 1 |
| Greens (Greens) | 5 | 18 | 1 |
| Christian Democrats (EPP) | 4 | 15 | 1 |
| Others | 4 | — | — |
| Total |  | 349 | 22 |

Source: *Info Memo 1* (Brussels: European Parliament – Directorate of the Press, 4 January 1995).